CONTEMPORARY
CRIMINAL JUSTICE PLANNING

CONTEMPORARY CRIMINAL JUSTICE PLANNING

By

HARRY W. MORE, Jr., Ph.D.
Golden Gate University
and
San Jose State University

and

MICHAEL E. O'NEILL, Ph.D.
Corporate Officer, Stonex, Inc.
San Jose, California
and
University of Southern California
Institute of Safety and Systems Management

CHARLES C THOMAS · PUBLISHER
Springfield · Illinois · U.S.A.

Published and Distributed Throughout the World by

CHARLES C THOMAS • PUBLISHER
2600 South First Street
Springfield, Illinois 62717

© *1984 by* CHARLES C THOMAS • PUBLISHER

ISBN 0-398-05009-0

Library of Congress Catalog Card Number: 84-2505

With THOMAS BOOKS *careful attention is given to all details of manufacturing and design. It is the Publisher's desire to present books that are satisfactory as to their physical qualities and artistic possibilities and appropriate for their particular use.* THOMAS BOOKS *will be true to those laws of quality that assure a good name and good will.*

Printed in the United States of America
SC-R-3

Library of Congress Cataloging in Publication Data

More, Harry W.
    Contemporary criminal justice planning.

    Bibliography: p.
    Includes index.
    1. Criminal justice, Administration of—United States—Planning.
I. O'Neill, Michael E.   II. Title.
HV9950.M67   1984   364'.973   84-2505
ISBN 0-398-05009-0

PREFACE

The planning process in criminal justice agencies is receiving increased attention, but is still highly fragmented and misunderstood. Planning gained a great deal of support when the Law Enforcement Assistance Administration was a viable organization, but since its demise, many planning agencies and units have ceased to exist.

Planning, consequently, has been less intense and is reactive rather than proactive. Planning, nonetheless, is an inseparable part of the management process and an essential ingredient of efficient administration. Nonexistent or incomplete planning can only lead to failure.

Successful planning calls for the active support and encouragement of policymakers. If planning is to play a vital role within an organization, policymakers must be committed to it and make this commitment known.

This text is designed to bring together the bits and pieces of criminal justice planning into a logical, practical, and useable framework.

The outline of the text follows the consistent sequencing of planning activities. Where appropriate, practical examples are set forth that clarify and illustrate specific planning activities.

The authors would like to give special thanks to Ronald F. Bykowski and Robert S. Blair for their initial work in criminal justice planning and to University Associates, Inc. and Justice Systems Development, Inc. for permission to reproduce parts of their works.

CONTENTS

CONTEMPORARY
CRIMINAL JUSTICE PLANNING

Chapter I

INTRODUCTION TO MANAGEMENT PLANNING

As one begins the study of criminal justice planning, it is immediately apparent that this is a recently created process and consequently is in its evolutionary stages. Even the concept that the criminal justice system is a system is challenged, and the concept that it is a series of processes linked together by the offender is set forth in this chapter. Each of the processes is described in terms of its mission. The need for criminal justice planning is established as the link that brings the individual processes of the criminal justice system together in such a manner as to harmonize the diverse individual efforts. The benefits of planning are described, as well as the process and steps to be used in criminal justice planning. The chapter concludes with a discussion differentiating between the different types of plans and the way they relate to the planning process.

CRIMINAL JUSTICE PLANNING—EMERGING BODY OF KNOWLEDGE

A decade ago phrases such as *criminal justice planning* or *crime-oriented planning* did not exist in the vocabulary of public officials. Few police, courts, and corrections agencies articulated what was desirable for their own agency, let alone what should be worked for in conjunction with other agencies.

In 1967, the President's Commission on Law Enforcement and Administration of Justice recommended that in every state and every city an agency of one or more officials should be specifically responsible for planning in crime prevention and control and encouraging their implementation. The recommendations of the President's Crime Commission reflected a concern for systemwide planning. This meant, at the very least, *ad hoc* coordination among police, courts, and corrections agencies so that policies implemented in one part of the system would not have an adverse effect on other components.

The creation of state and local criminal justice planning agencies and departments under the Omnibus Crime Control and Safe Streets Act of 1968 has given criminal justice planning a systemwide focus. The National Advisory Commission on Criminal Justice Standards and Goals encourages the development of criminal justice planning efforts and of allied governmental efforts that contribute to the planning process such as program budgeting,

3

intergovernmental emphasis on evaluation, measurement of government performance, and construction of integrated information systems.

Planning is becoming more than a concern over processing efficiency. It is becoming impact oriented. Restrictions in the costs, fear, and harm caused by crime are being planned for directly. A more sophisticated, long-range type of planning is now slowly being achieved. In addition, planning efforts are coinciding with the spread of program budgeting (budgeting by objectives) which, like planning, is future oriented. Finally, recent federal, state, and local funding of integrated information systems appears likely to give planners the data base they lack at present. Increased emphasis on performance measurement will be a probable result of the more abundant flow of information. Planners will be engaged heavily in the design and the use of evaluation efforts.

None of the developments described are advancing evenly in each state or unit of local government. Yet, these are national trends that cannot be ignored. The emerging criminal justice planner is the spearhead for these trends as he simultaneously creates and defines a new profession in the annals of the evolving criminal justice system.

THE JUSTICE SYSTEM

The current operation of the criminal justice system in the United States has not been successful in the prevention and control of crime. This failure is primarily due to a criminal justice system that attempts to decrease criminal behavior through a wide variety of uncoordinated and sometimes uncomplimentary efforts. The key components of the criminal justice system — the police, the judiciary, correctional institutions, and community-based social agencies — have varying degrees of responsibility for removing the causes of crime. These system components have responded to the current crime situation without sufficient understanding of their mutual responsibilities and common objectives.

This lack of understanding is manifested by the failure of each system component to take part in joint planning and action, and also by friction, conflict, and deficient communications. These failures result in ineffective crime prevention and control and inefficient resource utilization.

For example, the role of law enforcement is to arrest suspected offenders — their performance is partially judged by the number of arrests they make. They are not publicly judged on the quality of their arrests but the quantity. Therefore, if a law enforcement agency becomes overzealous in its arrest efforts, sight may be lost of the necessary evidence required to develop a good case resulting in a valid conviction. A common complaint voiced by prosecutors is the poor quality of case reports they receive from the police, thus making convictions almost impossible.

The prosecutor, on the other hand, is partially judged publicly by his success in obtaining convictions. A public defender or defense attorney, however, is judged by his success in getting suspected offender's charges dropped. Nowhere in this adversary process is either the prosecutor or defense judged publicly by his ability to apply justice. Rather, this is assumed to be part of the professional ethics associated with the personalities and character of these criminal justice system employees.

The courts carry the torch of being individuals, thus sentencing offenders as they see fit, as opposed to operating under a code of uniform sentencing policies. A court in one part of a county may give an offender a suspended sentence and ninety days probation for a minor marijuana possession charge, while another court in the same county will decree a year in the county jail as its sentence for the same charge.

Corrections personnel are torn between the philosophies of punishment and rehabilitation and wind up performing neither with any degree of success. They are further burdened with overcrowded conditions in antiquated facilities. Community-based corrections, an emerging offspring of the rehabilitation philosophy, is striving to prove its concepts. These constitute but a few of the frictions, conflicts, and miscoordinations that are representative of the criminal justice system. It is precisely these diverse interests, objectives, and turmoils that the planner must somehow harmonize in a directed effort for the reduction of crime.

This is further defined and explained by Glaser (1975) in his text on Strategic Criminal Justice Planning. He states:

> One implication of many recent criminal justice developments is that strategic planning cannot be done by any component within the system acting alone. This is evident from the probation subsidy experience, for example, which drastically affected both courts and institutions. It is also evident in police diversion of juveniles from the courts. Another example is in the effort of crime prevention agencies to provide trade training as a condition for pretrial release for those whose poor employment record makes them unable to post bail as well as poor risks for unconditional recognizance. All these practices indicate that changes in police activities will affect courts, that changes in the courts will affect both police and correction, that changes in correction will affect police and courts, and that any effective crime prevention measures will affect all criminal justice agencies. Because of this interdependence of parts—because, though poorly coordinated, criminal justice is indeed a system—strategic planning is best done by government agencies that are superordinate to police, courts, corrections, and prevention agencies, though receiving advice and information from all of them.

The criminal justice system as defined for the planning model in this text consists of four basic elements. The first element, and the largest in population and scope (the originator of the remaining elements of the system), is the society or environment that the system serves. Within this society, which is usually a county in structure, are the subelements: the crime victim, the offender, and the formal criminal justice system including police, courts, corrections, and private agencies.

Figure I-1 pictorially displays this concept of the criminal justice system. Within the boundaries of a given society, a law violation takes place. The output of this violation is usually a victim and an offender. Sometimes, as in the case of victimless crimes, the offender and victim are one and the same.

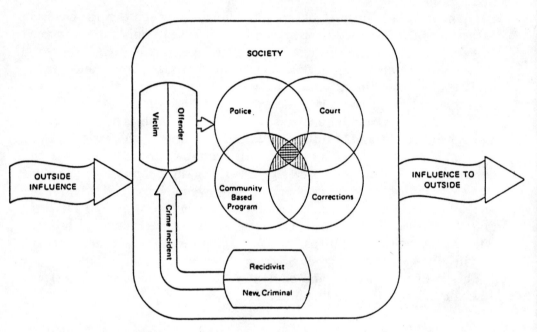

Figure I-1. Elements of the criminal justice system.

OBJECTIVES/GOALS

The police are responsible for the maintenance of social order within the constitutional and ethical restrictions set by the society. As illustrated in the following (*The Urban Police Function*, 1972), the mission generally is as follows:

1. To identify criminal offenders and criminal activity and, where appropriate, to apprehend offenders and participate in subsequent court proceedings.
2. To reduce the opportunities for the commission of some crimes through preventative patrol and other measures.
3. To aid individuals who are in danger of physical harm.

4. To protect constitutional guarantees.
5. To facilitate the movement of people and vehicles.
6. To assist those who cannot care for themselves.
7. To resolve conflict.
8. To identify problems that are potentially serious law enforcement or governmental problems.
9. To create and maintain a feeling of security in the community.
10. To promote and preserve civil order.
11. To provide other services on an emergency basis.

POLICE

The specific methods and operations used to satisfy these responsibilities vary in individual societies according to the local policies of law enforcement officials, their perception of their role, the interest of elected officials, and social pressures within the community.

The development and establishment of objectives is one of the most critical steps in the planning process.

The following serves to illustrate a number of specific objectives listed under several of the goals (Social Development Corp., 1973):

GOAL 1.

To identify criminal offenders and criminal activity and, where appropriate, to apprehend offenders and participate in subsequent court proceedings

Objective: Decrease the incidence of "resisting arrest" by _____ in FY 19_____-_____ as compared to FY 19_____-_____ and 19_____-_____.

Means: Implement a twenty-five hour training course through squad meetings (one-half hour twice a week) to run between January 1 and June 30, 19_____. Course material is to include practical training in law, methods, and techniques of arrest. (Methods would include training in planning arrests, timing arrests, etc.)

Implement an ongoing physical fitness/self-defense training program to be attended by all Operations field personnel.

Implement a training course concerning the psychology of arrest and the principals of persuasive speaking.

Measures: Percent decrease in charges of "resisting arrest."

Decrease in officer injuries in the commission of an arrest.

Decrease in citizen complaints evolving from arrests.

Objective: Bring about 20 percent increase in arrests regarding valid "in progress" crimes. Comparison periods to be FY 19_____-_____ with FY 19_____-_____.

Means: Develop a system of strategic manpower deployment based on intelligence data and MIS data aimed at providing personnel in high crime areas.

Develop systems of closing avenues of escape by response techniques established by a special study force and included in written form and squad room training. Systems to be enforced by responsible unit or responding supervisor.

Analyze information gathering techniques utilized by desk personnel and data dispatch procedures to seek improved means, through training, of dispatching personnel to crime scenes.

Measures: Decrease in response time to crime scenes due to improved manpower deployment SEU activity, response techniques, and data dispatch procedures.

Increase of at-the-scene arrests.

Increase of on-view arrests.

Objective: Increase burglary arrests by _____ over a sixty-day period.

Means: Organize special enforcement units to stake out high burglary areas identified on the basis of statistical data and police intelligence.

Coordinate all burglary reports with all other forms of police intelligence (Field Interrogation cards, suspicious circumstances reports, etc.) to develop comprehensive burglary dossiers to be provided to Selective Enforcement Unit and other operations personnel.

Provide for extensive interviews of all burglar arrestees by SEU personnel, to develop data on MOs location of stolen property, identification of additional suspects, etc.

Measures: Increase of burglars arrested over sixty-day period as compared to previous time periods.

Objective: Increase the percent of stolen property recovered by _____ over a sixty-day period.

Means: Utilize a Selective Enforcement Unit (SEU) to provide surveillance on known fences, pawn shops, and flea markets.

Use Investigative Technicians to compile comprehensive lists of stolen property emphasizing those items readily identifiable (i.e., serial or ID number, complete descriptions, uniqueness of items, etc.) for dissemination to SEU (Selective Enforcement Unit).

Provide extensive interviews of all suspected thieves arrested by SEU personnel.

Use Investigative Technicians to provide followup on all thefts emphasizing accurate property descriptions.

Measures: Increase of recovered stolen property over sixty-day period as compared to previous time periods.

The specific kind of special enforcement should depend upon an analysis of criminal statistics. This data should be fed into a Management Information System on a daily basis and analyzed monthly. The results of this analysis should determine the offensive actions of the department.

GOAL 2.

To reduce the opportunities for the commission of some crimes through preventive patrol and other measures

Objective: Reduce residential burglaries by ＿＿＿＿＿ during Fiscal Year 19＿＿＿ over previous fiscal years.

Means: Implement Operation Identification in ＿＿＿＿＿ homes in the community by the beginning of Fiscal Year 19＿＿＿ through homeowners' groups, Chamber of Commerce, community programs, and other civic organizations.

Measures: Measure the effectiveness of Operation Identification by the reduction of home burglaries in general and the rate of burglaries among homes participating in the program.

Recovery rate of property stolen from Operation Identification homes.

Means: Participate with city planners to review residential building codes to make recommendations regarding minimum standards for locks, windows and other security devices. This is the responsibility of the Planning and Research Section.

Measures: Evaluate the burglary rate in statistical reporting areas that represent the housing development incorporating the new security standards.

Means: Coordinate with school officials to identify potential truants and control truancy. Use Community Programs Technicians for this program.

Measures: A reduction in daytime burglaries.

Objective: Reduce commercial burglaries by ＿＿＿＿＿ during fiscal Year 19＿＿＿.

Means: Develop a program for merchants identifying common factors leading to community commercial burglaries and techniques available to combat those factors. Use Community Programs Technician and Police Services Technician Trainee for this program.

Prepare and gather supplementary brochures and visual aides for use in presentations to business groups.

Provide training PSTs to tour business establishments and make recommendations regarding burglary prevention techniques.

Provide follow-up checks with commercial representatives to determine what preventive actions have been taken by those businesses previously inspected.

Measures: Amount of decrease in burglaries committed at businesses adopting recommended crime prevention measures, and for those merchants who did not follow recommendations.

Significant percent of those businesses receiving a prevention inspection that will actually implement recommended crime prevention measures.

Objective: Reduce the number of repeated disturbance of the peace calls during the calendar year of 19_____.

Means: Implement a thirty-hour crisis intervention program for all patrol personnel between February 1, 19_____ and May 31, 19_____.

Develop a referral system of area agencies or individuals that provide various public services. This system is to be utilized in crisis intervention referrals by all members of the department.

Implement crisis intervention as a patrol function by June 1, 19_____.

Develop a follow-up procedure on referred cases with the P.S.T. IV Referral Technician assigned to the Community Relations Section.

Measures: A statistically significant decrease in repeat disturbance of the peace calls between June 1, 19_____ and December 31, 19_____ as compared to similar previous time periods.

Record the number of referrals and follow-ups made during the same reporting period.

GOAL 8.

To identify problems that are potentially serious law enforcement or governmental problems

Objective: Increase formal action taken on abandoned property over FY 19_____–_____ compared to FY 19_____.

Means: Assignment of Police Service Technicians to seeking out and reporting parties responsible for the abandonment of property such as automobiles and refrigerators.

Measures: Decreased incidence of abandoned property. Increase in reports.

Objective: Correct all hazardous conditions in public streets.

Means: Assign responsibility to Police Service Technicians to spot and immediately report any hazardous condition and its exact location for corrective action by the appropriate city department.

Measures: Percent increase in hazardous conditions corrected.

Objective: Increase student awareness in traffic and personal safety.

Means: Develop a citywide school safety program appropriate to the various grade levels for presentation by September 1, 19_____.

Utilize Police Service Technicians and Police Officers in presenting programs to all city school children.

Utilize outside firms and sources for equipment, materials, expertise, and instructors for presenting specific areas of safety to students.

Measures: Passing test scores on all material presented to insure retention of important points within the program and to allow certification.

GOAL 10.

To promote and preserve civil order.

Objective: Increase the level of departmental readiness to respond to the scenes of unusual occurrences.

Means: Develop and maintain a local emergency activation program that will have deployed all available personnel within a two-hour period at proper locations, equipped and informed as to their responsibilities in the operation. All personnel will know the purpose and procedures of this program.

Squad room training sessions reviewing personnel emergency action, reporting stations, and equipment checkoff list.

A field exercise simulating the call-up and deployment to specified locations and the performance of specific duties.

Operational guidelines and directives updated at least once annually and disseminated to all personnel involved.

Measures: The time required to call out and deploy fully equipped personnel to a simulated disaster area.

Written tests concerning assembly point, code designations, equipment location, and identification procedures for equipment release, and the individual's role and responsibility within the operation.

Objective: Increase departmental capability for controlling mass disorder threatening life and property.

Means: Organize and actively train an unusual occurrence force expert in crowd control, rescue techniques, and the suppression of a planned and prolonged armed attack.

Coordinate with adjoining law enforcement agencies and emergency forces (i.e., fire, ambulance) to establish unusual occurrence procedures and responsibilities.

Prepare advanced procedures for making and processing mass arrests consulting with the court system to determine areas of special concern.

Determine equipment responsibilities and provide all necessary means for the personnel to meet these responsibilities.

Measures: Degree of readiness of unusual occurrence force as determined through testing and drills.

Percent of necessary equipment available.

Increased understanding among all personnel, of procedures to be followed regarding personnel deployment, supervision, individual responsibilities, and equipment issue.

Understanding determined through testing and drills.

GOAL 11.

To provide other services on an emergency basis

Objective: Increase employees' capability in first aid and safety activities.

Means: Develop and implement a twenty-six hour first aid and safety course to be presented in fifty-two consecutive half hour sessions annually, beginning the week of July 1, 19_____. Components of this course will include the following:

1. Utilization of city swim lagoon and lifeguards to instruct departmental patrol personnel in lifesaving water safety.
2. Utilization of PG&E safety personnel to instruct departmental patrol personnel in electrical safety.
3. Utilization of departmental accredited instructors to provide refresher first aid, applicable to field unit use (i.e., choking, bleeding, respiration, shock).
4. Utilization of fire department personnel to instruct in rescue techniques.

Measures: Preinstruction and postinstruction exams to ascertain the percent increase in knowledge and ability gained through the training program.

Objective: Decrease by a statistically significant degree the response time to emergency calls while decreasing in the same manner personnel injuries and property damage sustained as a result of emergency responses. Comparison to FY 19_____–_____ with previous years.

Means: Develop and implement by April 1, 19_____ a sixteen-hour drivers training program designed to provide qualifications for all sworn personnel by July 1, 19_____. The program will utilize departmental instructors certified by the California Highway Patrol Driver Instructor six-week course.

Deploy the personnel in a strategic manner based on statistical data while continuously reviewing with personnel the most direct routes to various city locations.

Train Information Technicians in data gathering and radio procedures to direct field personnel utilizing the most complete location available (i.e., _____ address, the Smith Manufacturing Company or the Lexington Garden Apartments, east complex, southeast side).

Measures: Decreased response time (statistically significant).

Reduced police vehicle damage and personnel injury (statistically significant).

Reduced police vehicle damage and personnel injury (statistically significant).

Reduced incidents of personal injury and property damage due to emergency responses (statistically significant).

COURTS

The courts subsystem serves as a focal point or pivot upon which the criminal justice system revolves. The court's duties include the following:

1. The prosecutors office and/or the Grand Jury making the decision as to whether to file charges against an offender. This process includes the investigation and gathering of evidence.

2. The judiciary (plus juries as appropriate) deciding whether the offender shall be convicted of a crime.
3. The judiciary, with the advice of corrections, determining what is to be done with the offender after conviction.
4. Providing defense counsel to indigent defendants.
5. Determining which offender may be released on bail or own recognizance.
6. Performing appellate review and decision making.
7. Providing check and balance upon the executive agencies such as the police and other local government departments.
8. Performing both criminal and civil prosecution, judicial and defense functions.

Briefly, the court subsystem seeks conviction of the guilty and freeing of the innocent. The chief prosecutor and judicial seats within a given society are usually elective. Thus, their methods and operations are (theoretically) responsive to the surrounding social structure.

Within state court systems there is frequent jurisdictional overlap and confusion somewhat similar to that present among municipal and county police departments and county sheriff's agencies. The current state of disorganization within the police and court components does much to frustrate the interrelationship between the two.

As stated previously, the goals of each element of the system differ. Police define success by the number of arrests, the prosecutor defines success by the number of convictions, the public defender considers himself successful when he frees an accused offender, and the courts have taken it upon themselves to use the interpretation of laws as a means of legislation.

Police are accused of improper evidence gathering, giving poor testimony, and overly harassing parolees. Similarly, the courts are charged with dismissing too many cases because of minor technicalities. As a result, the interface between the courts and police is hindered by disorganization and lack of communication.

Following adjudication and sentencing, convicted offenders may either be fined, committed to jail, placed on probation, sentenced to the state correctional institutions, or given some combination of these penalties. Most of these possible results involve the correctional process, in an attempt to prevent future criminal acts by rehabilitating convicted offenders. It is a fragmented process, occurring at both the state and local levels involving both correctional facilities and community supervision, and under the jurisdiction of both law enforcement agencies (e.g., county sheriff) and correctional agencies (e.g., county probation departments and state corrections). The underlying assumption of the process is that correctional "treatment" should be reserved for those persons who pose a genuine threat to others, and that it should not be applied to nonserious offenders.

CORRECTIONS

Some of the duties that can be associated with corrections include the following:

1. Providing presentence investigation reports and information as appropriate.
2. Furnishing probation supervision.
3. Providing or facilitating the availability of official counseling/treatment as appropriate.
4. Maintaining custodial control of the offender and assuring his safety, welfare, and the safety of society.
5. Facilitating or furnishing custodial programs encouraging rehabilitation to include: vocational training, academic education, counseling, recreation, and other special programs.

Briefly, the correctional subsystem seeks rehabilitation of the convicted offender. Corrections, the least visible of the formal criminal justice system components, recently has been subjected to a new sense of urgency. This new pressure is guided by the principle that reformation, not incarceration or vindictive suffering, should be the purpose of penal treatment. These reform efforts have introduced the concepts of rehabilitation, diagnosis and classification, probation and parole into the correctional process.

The Executive Summary of the Commission (National Advisory Commission on Criminal Justice Standards and Goals, 1972, p. 43) summarizes this concept in the following comment:

> figures on recidivism make it clear that society today is not protected—at least not for very long—by incarcerating offenders, for many offenders return to crime shortly after release from prison. There is also evidence that many persons in prison do not need to be there to protect society. Many persons can serve their sentences in the community without undue danger to the public. There is substantial evidence that probation, fines, public service requirements, and restrictions are less costly than incarceration and consistently produce lower rates of recidivism. It is here that the challenge of the professional in corrections lies.

Related to the correctional phase of criminal justice are community-based programs. These include foster and group homes, guided group interaction programs, intensive community treatment programs, and halfway houses. Without a sense of "community," the crime prevention potential and sharing of mutual responsibility for the quality of criminal justice is unfulfilled. But much like the institutionalized elements of the system, community-based agencies are burdened with their own problems. These problems usually center around the conflict of acceptance and the lack of bureaucratic structure typically associated with a formal element of the system. For example:

1. Services available are unknown to either the offender or members of criminal justice agencies.
2. Many of the community agencies are in competition by duplicating services while needed services go unmet.
3. Because of the inherent nature of volunteer resources, the quality and reliability of services provided tend to be nonavailable or nonuniform.
4. Criminal justice agencies are conservative in their willingness to employ community-based programs because the responsibility for the offender always remains, by law, with the agencies and not with the community group.

A general failure to appreciate the intricacies, problems, and inter-relationship of criminal justice agencies has been a primary factor in the lack of cooperation that exists between criminal justice agencies and community-based programs.

JUSTICE SYSTEM AS A PROCESS

Perhaps our criminal justice system would better be described as a process. This process, then, involves the decisions and actions taken by an institution, offender, victim, or society that influence the offender's movement into, through, or out of the criminal justice system. Consequently this process also influences the system itself, either "horizontally," between one functional unit and another, or "vertically," within a single functional unit. Horizontal effects are a result of such factors as the amount of crime (which influences police and prosecutor activity and society frustration), the number of prosecutions (which influences court and defense attorney activities), and the type of court disposition affecting the population in correctional facilities and rehabilitative programs. Vertical effects are exemplified by court appeals (the number determining the work load of appellate courts) and by appellate court reversals of trial court decisions.

One authority (Nanus, 1974 p. 351) describes this by looking at planning from three levels of inputs and outputs. Figure I-2 illustrates this concept.

No one part of the criminal justice system can reduce crime by itself, nor can it afford to be insensitive to the concerns and objectives of the other parts. In actuality, the criminal justice system is of limited significance in preventing crime. Police on every city block, three times the existing number of prosecutors and judges, and redoing our correctional attitudes and programs will have but a limited effect on the total crime rate. Rather, the principal role of the criminal justice system must be to ensure justice,

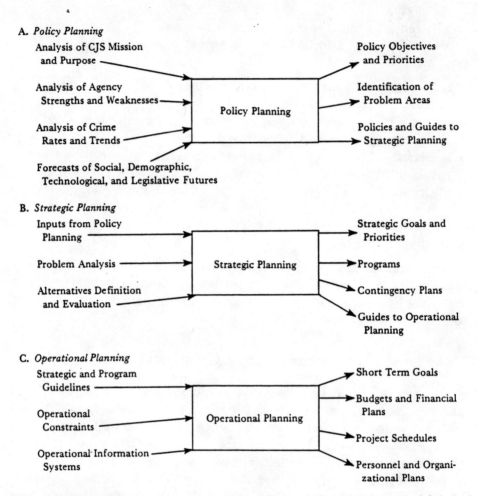

Figure I-2. Planning inputs/outputs. (Reprinted with permission from Journal of Criminal Justice, vol. 2, by Burt Nanus, "A General Mode for Criminal Justice Planning, 1974, Pergamon Press, Ltd.)

including fair and objective assessment coupled with the protection of constitutional rights.

The prevention of crime must begin much earlier than one's first contact with the system. As indicated by a national study (President's Commission on Law Enforcement and Administration of Justice 1967, p. 17):

> We will not have dealt effectively with crime until we have alleviated the conditions that stimulate it. To speak of controlling crime only in terms of the work of the police, the courts, and the correctional apparatus is to refuse to face the fact that widespread crime implies a widespread failure by society as a whole.

PLANNING PROCESS

The problems experienced by the elements of the criminal justice system have grown out of their organizational and administrative fragmentations. There is fragmentation among the components of the system, fragmentation within individual components, and fragmentation among political jurisdictions having various measures of authority over individual components. Systemwide criminal justice planning, including contributions by each agency of the system, provides a practical methodology to bring effective operation to the complex pursuit of criminal justice goals. Planning is the basic solution for any successful action seeking to integrate needs and to coordinate the fragmented segments of the criminal justice system within, between, and among its various components and elements.

PLANNING BENEFITS AND MANAGEMENT INTEGRATION

The scope of criminal justice planning will often transcend jurisdictional and individual agency responsibilities. Goals derived from a successful planning program will help delineate the relationships among the criminal justice agencies and the related public and community programs. These goals can frequently be directed toward multiple agency or even regional programs in an effort to reduce duplication of effort and attack crime on a more comprehensive front.

All elements of the criminal justice system should be included in the planning process in order that the resulting goals will be realistically related to the needs of the society. This does not mean that individual agencies should not do their own planning. In fact, just the opposite is true. It means that agency plans must be coordinated to assure nonconflict in furthering the system towards its established goals. Generally, criminal justice planning will encourage each component to more effectively identify its own particular problem areas. Planning will provide framework for determining priorities, encourage consideration of alternative courses of action, and assist in the anticipation of problems, thereby permitting the system component an opportunity to become goal and objective oriented rather than system maintenance oriented.

More specifically, planning for criminal justice activities facilitates the following listed items:

1. *Improved unity of purpose among the Criminal Justice components and the units that comprise the components.* Current expressed objectives of criminal justice components (or units within the components) often conflict. Police often view their primary purpose as to get the criminal off the street, yet corrections officials may see their role as one of rehabilitation, in which

locking up a criminal has little positive value for the individual. Similar examples can be cited between departments in a criminal justice agency. The administrative division in a police department is concerned with maintaining neat, accurate, and readily accessible files necessitating use of the patrolman's time in preparation. The patrolman, on the other hand, feels "paperwork" is wasting his time compared to "crime fighting." Somewhere between the police and corrections are the courts, trying to ensure a fair law application to all who are measured against it. However, the courts have sometimes worked at cross purposes to both police and corrections when recognizing the rights of groups and individuals as opposed to society at large. This is illustrated by recent Supreme Court decisions concerning the rights of the accused. A cooperative, comprehensive effort by all criminal justice components and units will help to identify their common interests and establish the direction in which the administration should proceed.

2. *Improve coordination of effort between and within political jurisdictions.* Many local governments are approaching insolvency because they are besieged on one side for reduction or leveling off of the tax rate and on the other by the citizen's desire for increased and improved services. Criminal justice planning, while not directly providing tax relief, can promote coordination among local jurisdictions, components within jurisdictions, and units within components leading to the more efficient allocation of resources (such as streamlining unnecessary duplication of services), thereby reducing public expenses. A direct product of planning is a budget and schedule by programs that can be evaluated by preestablished criteria for success or failure.

3. *Increased positive community involvement.* In addition to educating the public, involvement of the citizenry at certain stages of the planning process serves to provide a more constructive community relationship with criminal justice agencies. Improved citizen cooperation for both preventing and controlling crime can be expected if citizens are involved in pointing out problems and issues and in reviewing and suggesting solutions. Most regional planning efforts established by the Crime Control Act of 1968 have active citizen-at-large members participating on their regional planning boards. Also, recent nationwide Criminal Justice Standards and Goals efforts have encouraged citizen participation in the planning process. Additionally, citizen resources can be coordinated to implement community-based programs to relieve some of the criminal justice agency work load. Other benefits associated with planning to be realized particularly by the agencies employing the process include the following:

1. Identification and analysis of problems at departmental and agency levels.

2. Recognition of needs through assessment of existing resources.
3. Providing a method to define goals that can alleviate problems.
4. Establishing a framework to guide the assignment of priorities for allocating resources.
5. Encouraging the consideration of various courses of action for reaching a goal and help in the selection of a preferred choice.
6. Establishing formats for information reporting at each planning level.
7. Displaying milestones of accomplishment by which to judge progress.
8. Furnishing information to those who are involved in the design making process.

Planning can also provide rewards and benefits to the practitioner in the criminal justice system. These benefits are listed without ranking in order of importance.

Planning Can Improve Your Supervisory Style

Those criminal justice supervisors with ambition and talent are usually being groomed for better jobs and greater responsibilities, with a premium being placed on those who can organize and plan an activity. If you are aiming to be part of this select group, your methods of organizing the work effort may determine the extent of your potential for managing more complex activities.

Self-imposed Commitments Give You Confidence

It might sound strange to refer to making commitments as having beneficial attributes, yet, under planning methods, it is you who sets the unit goals to which you are pledged and makes the commitment by subordinates to accomplish given work loads that make it less a personal commitment than one of overall unit participation. Thus, you gain confidence from your plans because better control is in effect under them, and you continually see how actual results conform to planned actions. When someone else makes these commitments for you, goals may be imposed of an unsympathetic nature that can create apprehension regarding the achievability of them. Bear in mind that each revision to your work plan is in essence a chance to change to more realistic commitments.

Planning helps to integrate the management function. One authority (Wilson, 1974, pp. 4-5) describes the process as follows. Plans provide the broad base upon which much of management's philosophy is predicated and upon which the other management functions derive their meaning and purpose. Thus, they are integrated or united with the purposes in a plan.

This is partly illustrated in Figure I-3, where under the umbrella of a work plan, a number of things occur more or less in a simultaneous fashion: (a) guidance is furnished on the functions and goals of the unit, (b) this guidance provides for more interaction between the management functions as related to the goals or common purpose, (c) the cycle of activity (functions) does not lose this common purpose, even under the influence of internal or external factors in play, and (d) the results that do occur are subsequently fed back to the plan for comparison and evaluation with whatever progress the plan purported to achieve in any given period of time. Thus, you have a confirmation of the continued guidance from that plan or that some revisions need to be made.

It is possible that during the preparation stages of the plan, planning, programming, budgeting, staffing, organizing, assigning tasks, etc. may interrelate or occur simultaneously.

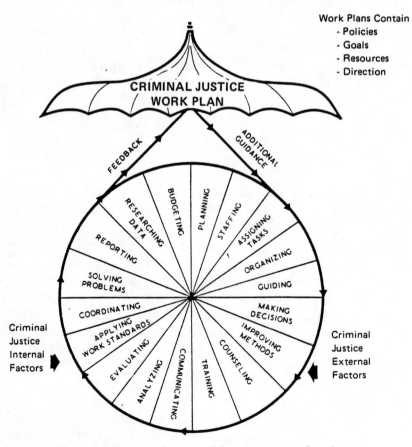

Figure I-3. Integrated nature of the management functions.

Once the plan has been implemented, organizing, guiding, training, counseling, assigning tasks, coordinating, applying work standards, etc., also interact with each other. These activities must all relate to the plan itself for purpose and meaning.

When progress has been made and certain results are produced, you go through the processes analysing, evaluating, reporting, researching data, improving methods, etc., occurring in close relation to each other.

From the foregoing it would appear that planning might be the panacea to all problems; however, such is not the case. Planning does provide a warning mechanism to facilitate early problem identification that, when isolated, can be solved.

THE PLANNING PROCESS

Planning should be dynamic in nature and should be regarded as a continuing process—constantly in progress rather than beginning each spring and ending the following winter—without a defined end.

Planning must be regarded as an inseparable part of the management process. It is essential to good, efficient administration. Major functions of planning are the identification of deficiencies, opportunities, and threats to the criminal justice system.

The result of this process is the documentation of a comprehensive plan to report each major step and provide a blueprint for action as well as establishing the framework around which agencies and units of local government may concentrate their efforts. (See Figure I-3.)

Successful planning requires the active support and encouragement of policymakers. If planning is to play a vital role within an organization, policymakers must be committed to it and make this commitment known. Such a commitment implies the willingness to take actions and to improve one's environment, both internally and externally. Another ingredient of a successful planning process is that staff, responsible for planning, have the confidence of the major policymakers.

Planning requires a blend of planning-oriented and operational staff, properly selected, to bring a broad spectrum of expertise and knowledge to the system. Generally, such a group can be more constructive since individual nonobjectivity becomes more difficult, and self-serving findings are less likely to result.

It must be remembered that there exists within most organizations a basic conflict between planning and day-to-day operations. One source of the irritation is planning's constant search for the identification and improvement of problem areas, which may be considered a reflection on the capabilities of operational management.

Planning needs to be conducted in the open and not in a vacuum. An aim of planners should be the constant education of themselves and others as to the purpose and content of planning efforts. It is particularly important to remember that key personnel must be kept informed and involved in the planning process. Further, planners cannot afford to be afraid of controversy because, by its very nature, a good planning process questions current activities, examines results, and creates controversy.

Maintaining objectivity is of primary importance, the lack of which often is the single greatest cause of error in any planning process and must be overcome if planning is to be successful.

There is also the need for developing applicable fiscal and information data bases. Current types of criminal justice fiscal and information systems were developed without planning in mind and leave much to be desired. However, they do serve as a base from which meaningful data may be constructed. A mistake many planning bodies make is the collection of too much useless data. To avoid this, it is important to determine what data are required, whether the data are available, and the collection techniques to be used.

The planning process must be the result of an orderly development. By its very nature a planning process should be specific, well-conceived, and flexible. It is necessary to remember that while the planning process is essential, it is the results of the implemented improvements that are of primary interest.

PLANNING STEPS

Within any planning process there exists a series of tasks necessary to its successful operation. The basic steps of the process set forth in this text are depicted in Figure I-4. Identifying problem areas is the first step. Other steps within this process are establishing goals and objectives, identifying alternative solutions, selecting the solutions, and implementation of planning and evaluation. Each of the steps, from the first to the last, represents a distinct link in the process.

Planning in the criminal justice system should begin with a perspective of the total system (prevention, control, adjudication, and rehabilitation). The performance of the complete system is examined with the intention of flagging problem areas.

Problem analysis cannot be overlooked, as it provides a focus for the planning process and is useful in maintaining coordination throughout the process.

The purpose of establishing goals and objectives is to set forth clearly the agreed aims of a particular group of criminal justice agencies, or of a single

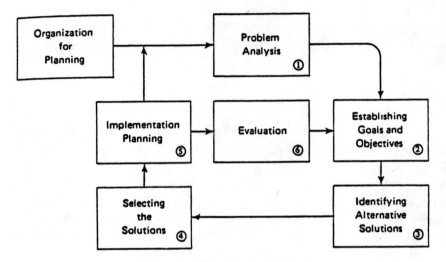

Figure I-4. The planning process.

agency of the system. Goal and objective setting is used to communicate the intent and direction that policymakers plan to take and the resources they may wish to commit.

Identifying alternative solutions begins with identifying the involvement of components and units of the criminal justice system in attaining the stated goals. From here, alternative plans are developed in detail, including schedules, constraints, resources required, impact, and organizational effects. During this step, criteria for selection among the alternatives are established.

The selection of the solutions may be done by a number of methods, including intuition and systems analysis, to name but two. In practice, selection is usually the result of considering numerous factors among which might be ability to meet stated goals effectively, probability of success, cost-effectiveness, and compatibility with present resources.

The next step in the process is the implementation of the chosen solution. This includes the development of detailed work plans.

The last step in the planning process is to monitor and evaluate the planning effort. The evaluation step is the process that closes the loop and permits one to determine

1. Whether the activity is on schedule and within the preplanned resource usage, and
2. whether it is accomplishing the goals and objectives it initially undertook.

Figure I-5 reflects an elaborate planning model suggested by the National Clearinghouse for criminal justice planning and architecture.

The remainder of this book will cover in detail each of the steps in the planning process. It will relate these examples. It is the intent of this text to provide the practical planner with operational tools for accomplishing his/her task.

PLANNING VERSUS PLANS

While the words are similar and interrelated, there is a fundamental difference between planning and plans. Planning is a basic organic function of management. It is a mental process of thinking through the desired and how it will be achieved. A plan is the tangible evidence of the thinking of the management. It results from planning. Plans are commitments to specific courses of action growing out of the mental process of planning. The planning process need not necessarily result in written plans; plans can be unwritten or expressed orally.

An illustration of the variety of the plans that might be prepared is illustrated in Figure I-6.

TYPES OF PLANS

By definition, a plan is a documentation of a projected course of action; thus, planning means determining what shall be done. There are many ways to classify plans. For example, the dichotomy of single-use plans and standardized plans. Single-use plans lay out one course of action to fit a special situation and are used up when the objectives are satisfied. Once designated, standing plans are used continuously with periodic updates (sometimes called a master plan or comprehensive plan).

Another classification refers to relative time intervals anticipated by plans: short-range plans and long-range plans. Short-range plans tend to have relatively inflexible goals. These goals should be made compatible with and unified by long-range goals. Long-range plans, which have more flexible goals, are not so well-defined in procedure. As we move up the hierarchical scale, the next classification of plans are strategic and tactical plans. Strategic planning is the process of determining the major goals and objectives of a criminal justice agency and the policies and strategies that will govern the acquisition, use, and disposition of resources to achieve those goals and objectives. The strategic planning process includes missions or purposes, if they have not been determined previously, and the specific objectives that are sought by an agency. Although the strategic plans are usually long-range, they can be short-range. In this area, we are dealing with the major, the most important and basic objectives, policies, and strategies of an element of the criminal justice system.

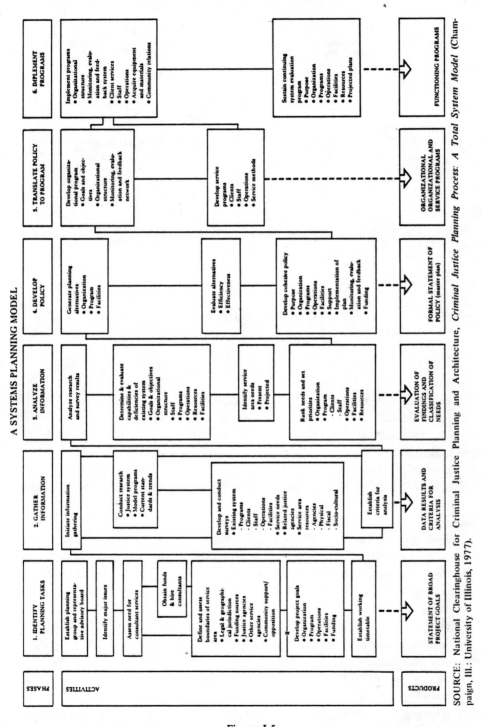

Figure I-5.

SOURCE: National Clearinghouse for Criminal Justice Planning and Architecture, *Criminal Justice Planning Process: A Total System Model* (Champaign, Ill.: University of Illinois, 1977).

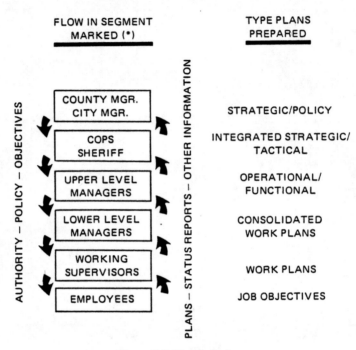

Figure I-6. Types of plans.

Tactical plans, on the other hand, relate to lower management levels. They are usually done on a periodic cycle that is on a fixed time schedule. Tactical planning is normally accomplished in greater detail and considers fewer alternative solutions. Uncertainty is less in tactical plans. Tactical planning problems are more structured and often repetitive in nature. They are usually the short-range type but can be long-range. Tactical plans should fall within parameters of strategic plans and usually entail greater details that are easy to evaluate.

A tactical plan for a police department might include a procedure for handling the looting of downtown merchants' shops during a general civil disorder. The strategic plan, on the other hand, would be comprised of many tactical plans and be a total coordinating procedure for the handling of civil disorders.

The last order of plans concerns the direction in which planning and solution implementation is to be expended. The first category is crime-oriented planning, which approaches criminal justice problems by considering subproblems categorized by the type of offense. In order to effect a reduction of crime, the planning effort must be specifically directed toward that end. Crime-specific planning is an attempt to develop strategies and tactics to overcome known crime problems and rapidly identify emerging crimes.

The counterpart of crime-oriented planning and the second category is system improvement planning and plans. These are plans that are created to produce improvement in the facilities, process, or manpower of the criminal justice system, whose improvement may or may not directly relate to the crime reduction process. There comes a point, for example, where a new jail must be built, not because it may reduce crime, but because of safety and humane factors toward inmates and responsible guards. Other examples include communication and management information systems. The foregoing discussion of plans and their relationship to one another are summarized in Figure I-7.

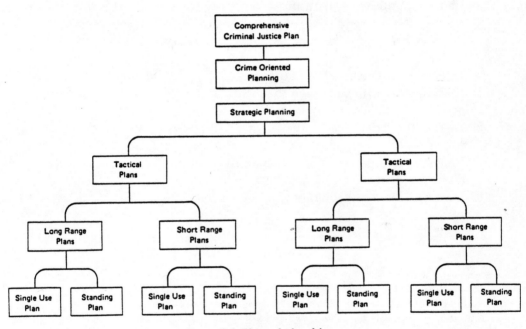

Figure I-7. Plan relationships.

The planning process and methodologies illustrated in the text are applicable to each of the foregoing types of plans described. The remainder of this text focuses on the planning process. The reader should determine the type of plan that meets his agency's need and initiate the appropriate planning process.

The criminal justice system defies a clear-cut definition, complicated by the roles and responsibilities of its several elements. We soon realize that the system is a nonsystem that functions as a process. Planning then provides a primary method by which this process can be harmonized to insure that common or nonconflicting objectives are being attained by each of the systems elements, components, and units. Further, we learn that planning provides an invaluable tool for the criminal justice administrator, assisting him in the timely and effective allocation of resources based upon the logic of need.

The basic steps of the planning process were discussed, and a differentiation is made between plans and planning. This chapter sets the stage for the remaining chapters in this text and should be clearly understood.

TOPICS FOR DISCUSSION

1. Discuss the role of the criminal justice system in our society.
2. Name the influences that impact a county level criminal justice system.
3. Discuss the consequences of justice system conflict between the major components—law enforcements, courts, corrections, and community-based activities.
4. Differentiate between the planning process and the scientific process.
5. Discuss what is meant when the criminal justice system is described as a process.
6. Discuss the difference between crime reduction and system improvement planning.
7. Relate your experiences with a planning process used in areas other than criminal justice.
8. Describe the types of plans and how they effect the criminal justice system.

REFERENCES

Ackoff, Russel L. *Creating the Corporate Future: Plan or be Planned for.* New York: Wiley, 1981.

Ackoff, Russel L. *A Concept of Corporate Planning.* New York: Wiley and Sons, 1970.

American Bar Association. *The Urban Police Function.* Chicago: American Bar Association, 1972.

Beer, Stafford. *Brain of the Firm.* New York: Wiley, 1981.

Cleland, David I., and King, William R. *Systems Analysis and Project Management.* New York: McGraw-Hill Book Co., 1968.

DeGreene, Kenyon. *The Adaptive Organization: Anticipation and Management of Crisis.* New York: Wiley, 1982.

Drucker, Peter F. *Management-Tasks, Responsibilities and Practices.* New York: Harper and Row, Publishers, 1974.

Eastman, George, editor. *Municipal Police Administration.* Washington, D.C.: International City Management Association, 1969.

Kazoroski, Ron. Formulation of goals in law enforcement agencies. *Police,* 8:62, 1980.

Nanus, Bert. A general model for criminal justice planning. *Journal of Criminal Justice,* 2:345, 1974.

National Advisory Commission on Criminal Justice Standards and Goals. *Executive Summary.* Washington, D.C.: G.P.O. 1974.

President's Commission on Law Enforcement and the Administration of Justice. *The Challenge of Crime in a Free Society.* Washington, D.C.: G.P.O., 1967.

Social Development Corporation. *Use of Manpower in a City Police Department.* Bethesda, Social Development Corporation, January, 1973.

Wilson, Charles. *How to Develop and Apply Work Plans.* Washington, D.C.: G.P.O., 1974.

Chapter II

ORGANIZING FOR EFFECTIVE PLANNING

Every department (whatever its size) needs and utilizes planning, whether the process is recognized as planning or not. In the large metropolitan departments this task is often handled by a specialized group of highly trained, well-paid individuals. In other departments, the planning function is usually handled by the chief or a deputy. The difference is quantitative. There is equal need for planning in both large and small departments; only the volume of activity and the form it takes differ.

Why does every department need planning? No situation is static. Even in the smallest community manpower needs, operating costs, crime rates, the regulatory work load, and public service requirements change with time. Communities grow in population size or, in some cases, diminish. And even where no noticeable change takes place in the size of the community, changes in composition of the population occur. Changes in age and sex, changes in the way people earn a living, changes in the income status of residents, and physical changes in the community all are factors affecting law enforcement.

The chief executive officer whose department keeps pace with the community must engage in a constant process of evaluation and revision. When it becomes necessary to request additional manpower, this officer must be in a position to go before the local legislative body and justify that request. When additional equipment and facilities or funds for training are needed, they must be explained in factual terms, meaningful to those who make decisions as to the allocation of public funds.

This requires planning. The financial support and cooperation from legislative and administrative bodies that is essential to effective performance can best be obtained on the basis of factual information, relating operations to changes in the community. The chief must be able to show evidence of the need for action, to evaluate alternative methods of meeting that need, and to present recommendations forcefully by demonstrating that requested funds will be purposefully directed to the solution of real problems. The rapid increase in the cost and complexity of criminal justice in recent years has made systematic planning a necessity in even the smallest communities (Ashby, LeGrande, and Galvin, 1968).

An important responsibility of top management in all but the very smallest criminal justice agency is to organize planning techniques. Because all operational supervisors have planning responsibilities and most staffs also become involved in agency planning, decisions must be made about which duties should be assigned to which people, what authority each should have, and what problems the planner should anticipate.

In addressing the planning program in most police agencies, it currently may be found to range from nonexistent to highly sophisticated. For the most part the existing planning is performed by the chief or a staff member. A separate planning unit has not been formed.

The National Advisory Commission on Criminal Justice Standards and Goals specifically recommended that all police departments with seventy-five or more personnel should establish a planning unit staffed by a minimum of one employee whose full-time responsibility is intraagency planning and coordination of planning activities.

In smaller agencies, the Commission recommended that one employee should be responsible for administrative planning or the chief should perform the planning function (Commission, 1973).

EXECUTIVE RESPONSIBILITY

Effective criminal justice planning will not occur (even in departments with a formed planning unit) unless the chief executive officer strongly supports such an effort. Lip service rather than commitment will result in failure.

Executive support must be an actuality, not a myth. Every member of the organization should be aware of top management support. Regretably, numerous criminal justice agencies today do not have the support of top management (Steiner, 1969).

One expert (Mace, 1965) stated:

> Probably the single most important problem in agency planning derives from the belief of some chief operating executives that agency planning is not a function with which they should be directly concerned. They regard planning as something to be delegated to subordinates who can do without responsible participation by chief executives.

Fortunately, not all chief executive officers fall into this classification. Increasing numbers of chiefs have a firm grasp on the importance and the primacy of their responsibility for planning. Planning provides the agency head with a process that gives direction to the agency and facilitates the attainment of goals. Acceptance of their task reduces goal conflict and keeps all subdivisions working for a common purpose.

Certainly the chief may delegate some degree of responsibility for planning, but the ultimate responsibility for coordination and control must remain with the person in this top position. As the agency increases in size, this becomes increasingly difficult as the chief executive officer is called upon to deal with increasingly complex social, political, and technical developments (Steiner, 1969).

But even when a chief executive accepts the importance of the role in planning, it is not always easy to find the time to do what is required with confidence, or to determine precisely what one's role ought to be in the many activities and with the many individuals and groups concerned with planning. There is no single way to discharge properly the many responsibilities in planning. The issues are subtle, complex, and vary much from one agency to another, from one executive to another, and over a period of time.

BARRIERS

The chief executive's ability to clarify and discharge the planning role are limited by a number of barriers, including limited available time, a temperament unsuitable to planning, and the difficulties in dealing with everyday pressures generated by the position.

A paradox of contemporary executive life is that the burdens and work week of the average manager have expanded considerably. The political and social pressures that impinge upon the managerial position today were unknown a few decades ago. These factors, plus internal organizational variables such as unions, reinforce and compound the executive load. Unfortunately the complications in management increase at a faster rate than the development and application of tools and techniques to lighten the tasks (Steiner, 1969).

Many executive officers have risen to the top position through one or more functional areas. The head of a law enforcement agency generally will have extensive operational experience from patrol or investigations, and occasionally traffic. In a probation department, functional experience is normally obtained through supervision or presentence investigation.

Allowing for individual variance, previous experience may provide the basis for bias in favor of street experience. This is especially true if the experience is the repetitive type instead of accumulative. Consequently, the pattern of thinking about problems may not be compatible with the need for overall agency planning.

The individual who has spent the better part of their career confronting problems that require an instantaneous response may find it most difficult to shift to a response pattern that requires a broad and comprehensive planning approach (Steiner, 1969). It is easy to see how an executive officer who has successfully reacted to short-range situations and has never had the opportunity to form comprehensive long-range plans could, upon attaining high rank, fully accept responsibility for agency planning, but never be capable of fully discharging the task (Steiner, 1969).

Lack of experience with or trepedation in conducting comprehensive planning should not be an excuse for neglecting the task. Such a problem can be surmounted if the chief will share the task with another manager or someone on the staff who is capable and motivated to complement the managerial style and interests of the chief executive officer.

Inherent to the chief executive office are numerous dilemmas that can be barriers to the assertion of a strong leadership position and positive participation in planning. On the one hand, a chief must create an organizational milieu having a reasonable degree of stability and routine response to events and situations. An agency will be ineffective if standard operating procedures are lacking and instability prevails.

On the other hand, the chief must be instrumental in preparing an organizational response to the changing demands placed upon it by the political and social environment.

The competing needs of stability and change must have a balanced response. The chief should strive to be a conservative *change agent*. Events and people should be controlled, but never to the point where an employees initiative is stifled or inhibited. Comprehensive planning can create a positive control system that supports the growth and development of not only the agency but its personnel.

TOP MANAGEMENT SUPPORT

It is of primary importance that the chief executive officer positively support criminal justice planning. Verbosity is not enough. It does not take one long to know whether the *boss* supports planning or not.

Effective planning can only exist in a positive agency environment. Results are clearly achievable when *top management* lets everyone know that planning is an integral part of the managerial process. Top management must accept the proposition that planning is an identifiable and controllable function that is not only central to organizational health but essential for growth and development.

Effective planning demands involvement by the chief executive and support from all levels of management. Such an organizational environment will support the involvement of first line supervisors and some line personnel.

When one addresses the question of how much should the chief executive participate in planning, there is no simple answer. One authority suggests (Steiner, 1969):

For the first planning effort the chief executive must be deeply involved. As experience is acquired and more staff help is available, a chief executive will know better where and when to become involved in order to exert proper influence. The degree of involvement also will be influenced by the style of the chief executive, whether the person is a "loner" or a democratic-participative operator. Much will depend upon the size of an enterprise, its problems, personalities. . . .

The chief executive officer must strive for a balanced response to planning demands. Too much involvement will lead to the neglect of other managerial duties. Only the chief can determine the correct balance between an adequate or excessive participation in an agency's planning process (Steiner, 1969).

Effective planning done by or on behalf of top management must result in operational decisions. Needless to say, without decisions the planning process is incomplete.

Management's failure or inability to respond to properly prepared plans will weaken and eventually destroy staff efforts. Planners who never see the fruits of their labor will not be motivated to creatively respond to problems. Too many plans sit on shelves and collect dust as a result of being ignored by management.

This in no way suggests that top management should rubber-stamp plans. Depending upon the situation, it may be essential that the chief reject or alter the plan. Flexibility to situational demands is essential to survival in a dynamic and changing society. Executive officers are responsible for making planning decisions that are compatible with the mission of the agency and the achievement of organizational objectives.

ORGANIZING FOR PLANNING

The chief executive officer is responsible for the development and implementation of a planning system within the agency. In accomplishing this task, the chief should obtain the assistance and support of staff and line personnel. The chief has the sole responsibility to see that the planning system is appropriate to agency needs and that it is cost-effective (Steiner, 1969).

Size of the agency is of paramount importance. In small criminal justice agencies there is no choice; the chief executive officer will be required to do all the planning. It is just the question of the chief wearing another operational *hat.*

As an agency grows, the chief will have to obtain assistance in planning from line or staff personnel. In larger organizations (seventy-five or more) a planning unit is appropriate. Once that decision is made, the chief must make it clear to all agency personnel that the unit has top management endorsement and support. This in no way suggests that the chief become involved in the day-to-day operations of the planning process, but it does suggest that authority and responsibility are delegated and that the planning process becomes operational (Steiner, 1969).

It is essential that the chief executive officer appoint someone to the planning position who will vigorously develop and implement a planning program. If the planning position is delegated to a staff or line manager, the person selected should be someone who commands the respect of the organization.

If the individual appointed has previously failed as a line manager, or if the planning position is viewed as a demotion, or if agency personnel view the post as a *punishment* position, or if an incompetent person is given the job, the planning process is doomed to failure (Steiner, 1969).

There are many ways to divide planning responsibilities, but they are too numerous to detail here. Whatever choice, the chief executive must make sure that the planning system is understood by everyone in the organization and the responsibility of each manager is clear and concise. Organization for planning is very important, but as one expert says (Tilles, 1964):

> The formal distribution of planning responsibility is less significant than the degree to which the top executives of the company, and especially the chief executive, see themselves as significant contributors to the planning process.

There is no single organizational planning configuration that is suitable to all agencies, nor will one organizational pattern insure effective planning. Examination of both local and state agencies reveals that there are five basic classifications of formal planning organization. From the simplest to the most elaborate they are as follows (Steiner, 1969):

1. No formal planning exists at all. Planning is done, but it is a part of the duty of each executive, and no effort is made to formalize the process. This pattern is typical of many very small agencies with few managers.
2. Organized planning is done within a functional activity. The area can be administrative, operations, or finance. For example, planning in a police system may center in the patrol division, because crime evaluation is a function about which organized planning for such agencies may be developed.
3. A planning executive and organization may exist in the divisions of an agency or operating units in the field, but no planning staff exists at the central level. In such cases, the chief executive may serve as a central focal point for planning, aided by functional officers from headquarters.
4. A central headquarters planning department is created, but no planning executives or staffs are established in operating units. In such instances, of course, the planning department usually gets involved in detailed planning.

5. A planning executive and staff exists at the central headquarters and in each major division or operating unit.

PLANNING RELATIONSHIPS

The relationship of the chief executive to the planning staff is frequently one of the most misunderstood elements of the planning process. When the chief utilizes a line officer to perform the planning function, has an administrative assistant perform this duty, or appoints a planning head, the chief is, in actuality, extending the capabilities of the office. It is a process whereby the chief executive officer accomplishes assigned duties and responsibilities. It is a recognition that executive responsibilities extend beyond the capability and capacity of one individual (Steiner, 1969). It can be exceedingly difficult to define the exact relationship between the chief and any one person, unit, or functional area, but the task becomes increasingly complex as the agency becomes larger.

As an organization evolves, managerial roles must be clarified. Primary responsibility for this clarification rests with the executive officer. The chief should emphasize that a planning staff cannot and should not be asked to make agency plans. This task is a line responsibility—not staff. Planning units support and assist line managers in the preparation and development of plans.

It is readily apparent that even though all levels of management can and should participate in the preparation of plans, the chief cannot simply request that a plan be created and sit back and wait for the finished product.

If the chief abdicates responsibility for planning and allows the planning staff to make all decisions, the chief in many instances will be left in an untenable position. In one instance, if substantial changes become a prerequisite, it can be exceedingly expensive and will eventually result in a demoralized staff. The other side of the coin suggests that for the most part, if few or no changes are made, there is a substantial danger of the chief executive becoming a captive of the staff planners (Steiner, 1969).

If the latter choice is selected by the chief executive, responsibility is abdicated and the agency's mission is abrogated. Consequently, the agency's planning capability will deteriorate and eventually cease to exist.

One expert pointed out that (Cleveland, 1963):

> The most useable end product of planning is not a paper, but a person thoroughly immersed in the subject—a person whose mind is trained to act, having taken everything into account, on the spur of the moment. And that is why the ultimate decision-maker must actively participate in the planning exercise.

Management style exerts a strong influence on the relationship between line and staff personnel. An authoritarian manager may give an order based on specified objectives and will, in fact, dictate results. In some agencies, this has produced desired effects, while in others it has proven to be disastrous. If the chief executive does not articulate objectives, the planning staff will usually be at a loss to respond to agency and community needs.

A more positive working relationship is one where there is a continuous interaction between the chief executive officer and the planning staff (Steiner, 1969). Interaction between chief and planner encounters the normal interrelationship issues complicated by the special problems of planning. This is illustrated by a highly sensitive issue that arises between the chief and the planner—that of frank and open discussion. The chief executive operates from a position of prestige and power, thus allowing for a potentially dictatorial response pattern—*do it!*

The planner, in helping the chief fulfill agency objectives, may have a personal need to achieve and obtain recognition on their own behalf. The problem is that it is perceived as inappropriate to speak freely as if both individuals were operating from the same level.

This dilemma can only be overcome if each contributes to the planning process from a position of total mutual respect and confidence. It is a two-way street, demanding an adjustment by both (Steiner, 1969).

Planning units are labor intensive and thus impact on the budgetary process. Therefore, they can create problems rather than provide suggested solutions. This causes one to question the desirability of having such a department.

A planning unit can prove to be a major asset in agencies large enough to provide support. A planning unit that can successfully perform the functions described in this text can contribute significantly to goal attainment. This can be accomplished by the application of appropriate problem solving techniques and professional judgment. The result is the suppression of personal needs and the reduction of functional bias.

If a planning unit tries to assume sole responsibility for planning, its existence should be questioned. If the unit becomes abstract and abstruse in its performance and concerns itself with matters unrelated to management problems, it should be eliminated. In the event the planning function is used as an excuse for top management to avoid a planning responsibility, the unit should be dissolved.

TOPICS FOR DISCUSSION

1. Discuss the role of the chief executive in the planning process.
2. Describe how the chief executive's temperament affects the acceptance of planning.

3. Discuss the relationship of a chief executive to his planning department.
4. Discuss how to organize for planning.
5. Discuss the relationship of a planning department to the line and staff.
6. Identify the limitations in staff planning.
7. Describe the advantages of staff planning.

REFERENCES

Albanese, Robert. *Management: Toward Accountability for Performance.* Homewood, Illinois: Richard Irwin, 1975.

Ewing, David E. *The Practice of Planning.* New York: Harper and Row, 1968

Garmire, Bernard L., editor. *Local Government Police Management.* Chicago: I.C.M.A., 1977.

Haimann, Theo, and Scott, William. *Management in the Modern Organization.* Boston: Houghton Mifflin Co., 1974.

Hale, Charles D. *Fundamentals of Police Administration.* Boston: Holbrook Press, 1977.

Mace, Myles L. The president and corporate planning. *Harvard Business Review.* January--February, 1965.

More, Harry W., editor. *Effective Police Administration,* 2nd Edition. St. Paul: West Publishing Co., 1978.

Skoler, Daniel L. *Criminal Justice Organization, Financing, and Structure.* Washington, D.C.: U.S. G.P.O., 1978.

Steiner, George A. *Top Management Planning.* London: The Macmillan Company, 1969.

Tilles, Seymour. *Strategic Planning in the Multi-Divisional Company.* Boston: Boston Safe Deposit and Trust Company, 1964.

Chapter III

PROBLEM ANALYSIS
A Proactive Approach

S electing and formulating a topic for scientific investigation is usually very laborious. In fact, for many planners it is more difficult to formulate the problem than it is to solve it (Franklin and Osborne, 1971).

A well-formulated problem is an essential prerequisite before the researcher considers what data will be collected, what methods will be used, and what will be the nature of the analysis.

Some planners make the mistake of selecting a topic and then immediately starting data collection. This can mean that the planner will be faced with the task of formulating a problem after data collection (Selltiz, Jahoda, Deutsch, and Cook, 1959).

The purpose of this chapter is to introduce the reader to a problem analysis approach. Key problems can be identified and techniques can be utilized to resolve or control the problem.

NEED DETERMINATION

Of primary importance to the development of a plan is the realization that a need exists, or that there is at least adequate concern for the preparation of a feasibility study. Recognition of a need is the first step in the planning process. It is an important step, for when the real needs are being met, an organization (or in this case a criminal justice agency) will be performing at maximum ability or efficiency.

Since criminal justice agencies are nonprofit organizations, the realization of maximum performance may be somewhat elusive. Whereas a *company* has the definite goal of profit or loss, the *criminal justice agency* deals with people. The agency, therefore, must be cognizant of and responsible to community problems and needs.

The citizens of a community are the fundamental reference group for a police agency. All of us are familiar with public officials or police administrators who justify their policies by referring to *what the public wants*. However, in numerous instances there are substantial differences between the public's desires and the services rendered. One way of identifying the needs of citizens is to examine requests for police service (Whitaker et. al., 1980).

An example of the problem categories identified from calls for police service are presented in Figure III-1. The review of such data provides the planner with a starting point for specific problem identification.

Problem Category	Definition	Percent of Calls* (Rank)	
1. VIOLENT CRIME	One person injures another in a manner that involves potential criminal liability.	4%	(9)
2. INTERPERSONAL CONFLICT	Persons involved in a dispute or altercation.	8%	(6)
3. MEDICAL PROBLEMS	Persons who are ill or injured.	1%	(11)
4. NONVIOLENT CRIMES	Nonphysical injury in a manner that involves criminal liability.	14%	(2)
5. TRAFFIC	Dangerous or illegal operation of motor vehicle or motor vehicle accident or hazard.	21%	(1)
6. PUBLIC NUISANCE	Unpleasant or annoying circumstance.	10%	(5)
7. SUSPICIOUS CIRCUMSTANCE	Situations that citizens (or officers) perceive as potentially annoying.	5%	(8)
8. DEPENDENT PERSON	Persons thought unable to care for themselves.	1%	(12)
9. PUBLIC MORALS CRIME	Affront to legal standards of "right conduct.".	2%	(10)
10. ASSISTANCE	All other problem situations in which citizens request help in dealing with a problem.	12%	(3)
11. INFORMATION REQUEST	Person wants information from police.	11%	(4)
12. INFORMATION FOR POLICE	Person provides information to police.	6%	(7)
13. INTERNAL POLICE OPERATIONS	Police provide a service to police and no direct service is provided to citizen.	1%	(13)

*Calls for police service.

Figure III-1. National Institute of Justice. *Cutback Management in Criminal Justice.* Washington, D.C., G.P.O. 1982.

PROBLEM IDENTIFICATION

Problem identification can be initiated by establishing the boundaries of the problem. The general boundaries of a problem can be circumscribed by stating some demographic constraints identifying the parameters of the problem. For example, we are only concerned with the problems that are indigenous to police department X, county Y, or a given state.

A second general boundary consideration is to limit the problem development process to those areas where criminal justice planning professionals feel the problems may exist. Thus, the professional is given credit for knowing his business. Examples might include focusing attention on problem development related to (1) robbery, for a police department, (2) case load management, for a probation department, and (3) trial delay, for a court. Steven Isaac has identified a number of common mistakes in problem formulation that the planner should consider when engaging in the process of problem identification (Isaac, 1974).

CAUSATIVE RELATIONSHIP

Good agency planning is continuous. The planner, whether the chief executive or department head, should continue to feel the pressures of planning requirements. In a theoretical sense, no plan should appear in final form. Draft plans maintain the aura of flexibility, change, and improvement. The planning process does not even begin with a problem. Rather, there is an inescapable relationship among causative factors, problem and need determination, and plan development. Simply expressed, the relationship can be visualized as shown in Figure III-2. The agency planners must recognize this relationship in order to insure that the direction taken is toward the solution of real problems.

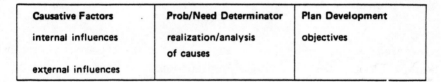

Causative Factors	Prob/Need Determinator	Plan Development
internal influences	realization/analysis of causes	objectives
external influences		

Figure III-2. Causative relationship.

DATA GATHERING AND ANALYSIS

The next step in the identification process is to develop the problem quantitatively as well as qualitatively. This involves researching and analyzing the problem area from the viewpoints of (1) statistics, or statistical analysis, (2) the people working in the department, and (3) the community.

As shown in Figure III-3, we are seeking those problems that are similarly identified by all three viewpoints; those identified by only two viewpoints; and those supported by only one viewpoint. These form our problem area list.

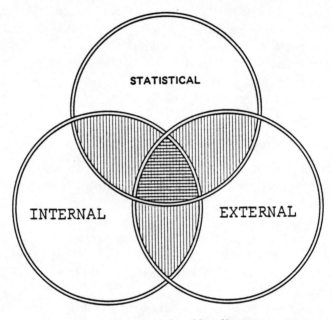

Figure III-3. Overview of problem list sources.

Statistical

Few areas rely more heavily on statistics than the criminal justice system and, specifically, the law enforcement profession. Trends in the types of crimes being committed, by whom, when, and where are meaningful, within limits, in the detection of criminal behavior. However, the interpretation of crime statistics must be handled carefully.

Crime statistics are only as useful as they are accurate. At the present time, a significant percentage of reported crimes are inaccurately reported. In addition, it has been estimated that only one-quarter to one-half of all crimes committed are ever reported. The incidence of unreported crime is highest in the inner-city areas where crime is the highest and where confidence in and respect for law enforcement is the lowest. Yet, this is precisely where the focus on the nature of crime and criminal behavior should be closest. Crime statistics must be reported in rates per population and must be related to population growth, income levels, education, and welfare rolls.

Because crime rates play an important role in society's fear of crime, and because an intelligent approach to crime statistics, to rates of recidivism, to case loads, and the like can yield worthwhile information, such information should be an integral part of problem identification (Hoffman, 1972).

Internal

The most obvious idea source for creating a problem list (identified as an internal influence) is the chief executive. Often the planner is not the chief or senior executive. When this is the case, utilization of the chief executive's knowledge as a potential source of ideas is a good idea in itself. A chief executive has spent a considerable amount of time observing the agency's performance from every aspect (having thought through possible problem areas and improvement needs). The chief is also the best source for obtaining a complete understanding of the criminal justice system's (as well as that agency's) goals and objectives. Consequently, when confronted with a need or problem, the ability to place it mentally in priority and provide the planner with considerable insight becomes possible.

Other senior management levels are also potentially excellent sources of ideas. They, relative to their own respective roles, can give the planner information about a unit's problems, function, capability, and limitations. Collectively or singularly (depending on the planner's need), management can be an extremely important idea source.

Another internal source is the agency's personnel. They deal with the day-to-day routine of agency operation, and often can see a problem developing (or existing unnoticed by higher levels of management).

There are several ways of recruiting the personnel's ideas. Employee suggestion boxes are a possibility. This method has been utilized by the private business sector and has met with some degree of success. In most cases, however, use of this method presupposes an attached incentive (varying from money, promotion, and esteem, to a combination of these). Another possibility would be for the planner to spend time talking individually with agency personnel. Good rapport can lead to voluntary suggestions or comments that could collectively be helpful in resolving a particular problem. In either case, continued openness by agency personnel will depend upon the planner's ability and sincerity in affecting changes where needed.

The planner can, through the chief executive, establish a built-in signal device to indicate certain problem areas without relying solely on total personnel participation. LeBreton and Henning (1961) call this *formal control:*

> The basic requirement for successful control consists of a set of standards for each significant item which reflects anticipated and desired performance, and on an acceptable range of variation from ideal performance.

Relating this to the criminal justice system, the method utilized in an agency's reporting procedure could conform to the formal control concept in helping to determine a problem area or need. In this case, submitting a report causes an automatic, or nearly automatic, response to take place.

Supervisors monitoring their areas of responsibility can discern a problem and report it to the planner.

External

When a criminal justice agency is preparing a problem list, input from the community is the most significant external source for gathering information. The community will react to their areas of concern. Since the community is generally so diverse, areas of concern pointed out by different groups or individuals will usually be issue oriented and aimed at particular departmental levels, i.e., policy/management, supervisorial, or functional. The planner can utilize community input as issues and problems arise within the system or a particular agency. Input of this type can be valuable in developing questionnaires used in attitude surveys that address the nature of the issue or problem.

Another informational source when developing a problem list is the collective judgment or opinion of individuals or groups concerned with the criminal justice system, including (1) elected representatives, (2) top administrators of other agencies, (3) staff and line personnel of other agencies, (4) community organizations, and (5) reports from local citizen's groups or those published in local newspapers. Meetings among agency executives and planners can be useful in the determination of problem areas, and can be a valuable idea source. This method works *if* the key players will participate and discuss their needs and desires openly. This type of planning discussion can be helpful in warding off interagency problems (within the criminal justice system).

The following example is indicative of what can happen where interagency planning is lacking. A lower court establishes a diagnostic project that will provide medical, psychological, exonomic, and educational information about a subject prior to sentencing. The court does not have the administrative capability to handle the project, so the court asks the probation department to manage the project. After a time, however, the chief probation officer comes to realize this additional workload is requiring numerous staff hours to satisfy the demands of the project. Then, as budget hearings commence, the local governing officials get upset when the chief probation officer adds a new position to the next year's budget. The impact of this chain reaction causes many people to be upset. Such situations need not occur with proper planning.

Another starting point in developing a problem list is the review of existing written descriptions of problems in the criminal justice system. Other common sources include the following:

1. Reports by other agencies within the criminal justice system including previous planning efforts by local criminal justice planning agencies.
2. Problems, goals, and priorities identified in state or national plans.
3. Recent articles, books, and other publications.

As the problem list evolves, from an analysis of statistical, internal, and external data, it is essential that the planner conform to a *standard* when presenting problem statements.

PROBLEM STATEMENT CRITERIA

The requirements for an acceptable problem statement should be clearly stated. For example, an acceptable problem statement

1. contains a narrative description (i.e., a statement, as precise as possible, that describes the nature and seriousness of the problem)
2. contains a quantitative description (i.e., an estimate of the magnitude or extent of the problem in numerical terms, based on available statistics or informed judgment)
3. is expressed from one of the following perspectives:
   a. types of crimes (e.g., narcotics, burglaries)
   b. criminal justice systems (i.e., the capability of the system to provide the type and quality of services required)
   c. offender profiles
   d. victim response
   e. community environment and resources (i.e., the contribution of community conditions to crime and to diversion of offenders; the effect of crime on life in the community)
   f. target areas
   g. transportation pattern
   h. modus operandi
4. is qualified by such information as
   a. data sources used (e.g., statistical summaries, surveys, expert opinions)
   b. geographical areas and population groups affected
   c. criminal justice components involved

SELECT AND ANALYZE SPECIFIC PROBLEM AREAS

Policymakers of the planning organization must be involved in selecting the problem areas that will be subject to further definition and analysis. The actual selection and analysis might be performed by one of the following groups:

1. By the planning staff, for review and action by policymakers. This approach is preferred when the planning staff is adequate in size

and experience and where it has the confidence and respect of the policymakers.

2. By a committee consisting of top administrators. These individuals usually offer the most experience and knowledge. As a group, they can be more objective because there is less individual fear of the critical conclusion, and the self-serving finding is less likely to emerge. As this group will be involved in directing the implementation of improvements, they should be involved throughout the planning process.

3. By a committee consisting of junior administrators for review and action by policymakers. This group is generally closer to operating detail and tends to retain more idealism and to be less compromising in judgments.

4. By outside consultants, for review and action by policymakers. Outside consultants can provide a valuable service in this diagnostic phase of planning, particularly if internal conditions are not suitable for an in-house effort.

Additional data must be gathered to measure and test hypotheses related to the selected problem areas. The choice of data collection techniques is determined by the following considerations:

1. The amount of pertinent data needed to statistically define the problem.
2. The resources available to collect data (personnel, time, files).
3. The accessibility of the data (whether the data exist in the proper format, at a convenient location).

As data are collected, there should be a continual review concerning the following:

1. Completeness—does the data cover all aspects of the problems?
2. Adequacy—are there enough data to make definitive statements about the problem?
3. Accuracy—have the data been recorded correctly?

It should not be expected that all data collected would meet such criteria, but any major inadequacies should be described and available to the decision maker.

GENERAL PROBLEM AREAS

A problem is an existing difficult and unsettled situation requiring a solution that will improve the situation and make it more acceptable. The following is an example of a problem:

The use of dangerous drugs and narcotics has increased to severe proportions in a specific community.

The next step is compiling a complete list of general problem areas. This list provides the basis for selecting and documenting the major problems facing the agency or department.

A typical list of problems might include the following:

1. Rapid change in expectations of criminal justice.
2. Ineffective prevention and deterrence.
3. Rising crime rate.
4. System overhead due to traffic violations, intoxication, and other minor offenses.
5. Fragmentation and duplication of criminal justice activities.
6. Antiquated management practices.
7. Statutes that hinder improvement.

MAJOR PROBLEM AREA

The general problems must then be listed according to their importance. The problem that *heads* the list then becomes the major problem confronting the agency. Figure III-4 is a sample major problem statement that addresses the use of dangerous drugs and narcotics.

The use of dangerous drugs and narcotics has increased to severe proportions in our community

1. There are limited educational programs for youth and adults on the hazards of narcotics and dangerous drugs.

2. The drug arrest rate for juveniles has increased 65% in three years from 20 per 1000 to 33 per 1000.

3. The drug arrest rate for adults has increased 37% in three years from 30 per 1000 to 41 per 1000.

4. Narcotics and drug abuse cases now comprise 36% of the court calendar or 604 of 1680 cases.

5. Treatment programs for narcotics and dangerous drug users have been notably unsuccessful with a 25% revocation rate.

6. Treatment programs provided by resources outside of the criminal justice system are inadequate.

Figure III-4. Problem statement for the use of dangerous drugs and narcotics.

The output of prioritizing general problems is the documentation of all major problems, thus serving two primary purposes: (1) the establishment of a focus for planning activities, and (2) a means of communicating among planners, officials, and the public. Such a format allows for the objective review and analysis of major problems. Decision makers are presented with documented analysis of problems that facilitate the budgetary decision process.

CONSTRAINTS ON SOLVING MAJOR PROBLEMS

The final task is the acknowledgment of constraints, or external forces (uncontrollable), that will limit the success of dealing with the major problems. Examples of these constraints which will determine the feasibility of an alternative improvement are the following:

1. Technical—What new equipment, special skills, or new operations are required?
2. Organizational—What is the organizational impact on the agencies affected in implementation? What is their reaction?
3. Social—What is the expected public reaction and participation?
4. Related programs—What are the difficulties in coordinating with other related programs?
5. Economic—How much of the available resources will be consumed?
6. Legal—What legislation is required?
7. Political—What political factors will impact upon implementation?
8. Demographic—Will implementation have a general effect or be more selective?
9. Geographic—What is the expected scope of impact in relation to the above?

It is important for the planner to be aware of the constraints a plan is likely to engender. Not that the planner must yield to the pressures of a few, but neither should the process be a sole source endeavor.

PROBLEM PARAMETERS

A planner who begins to utilize any type of statistical analyses must be mindful of the degree of involvement contemplated and the level of sophistication required to obtain needed information. In other words, jurisdictions and criminal justice agencies come in all sizes, and statistical analyses vary from a simple percent to factor analysis and multiple regression techniques. Generally speaking, the more worthwhile information is obtained by continued effort; however, the degree of difficulty increases also. The planner's own capability must be considered where sophisticated techniques are to be utilized. Possibilities for the need of outside resources, i.e., consultant services, should be evaluated.

There are some simple, generally acceptable statistical analysis approaches to problem identification. These take the form of the traditional approach to the planner's needs. Five basic problem parameters are easily obtained and will provide the planner with an understanding of important problem areas:

1. Magnitude.
2. Rate of change.
3. Seriousness.
4. Location.
5. Who.

What is being asked is the following:

1. What is the extent of the problem?
2. How is the problem changing (increasing or decreasing), and how fast?
3. How many people does the problem affect, and how does the problem compare with similar problems in other locations?
4. Where does the problem occur: what beat, city, county, or agency is the greatest contributor to the problem; where is it growing at the fastest rate; where is it most serious?
5. Who is causing the problem—generally speaking?

Magnitude

The magnitude of a problem can be determined by computing the percentage it represents in terms of the whole. For example, if out of 15,000 crimes reported there were 4,000 burglaries, then burglaries represent 27 percent of the total. ($4,000/15,000 \times 100 = 27\%$). Magnitude gives the planner a rough picture of the extent of the problems in relation to other crime problem areas.

Rate of Change

This parameter indicates how the problem is changing over a period of time. Small variations showing increases or decreases are expected on a yearly basis. What the planner is looking for here are some significant changes. Using the same example, say there were 4,500 burglaries the year before, then the difference divided by the previous year figure (in this case 4,500) gives a rate of change for that period. Four thousand burglaries (current year) minus 4,500 burglaries (previous year) = − 500 burglaries. The formula generates the percentage rate of change: − 500 (difference)/4,500 (previous year) × 100 = −11 percent rate of change. In this case, a decrease of 11 percent over the previous year.

Relative Seriousness

This parameter tells the planner, on a comparative basis, the extent to which one community faces a problem by comparing it to another. The community may be another jurisdiction of similar size, or a much larger one, as a county or state. It can also give a rough idea of how many people are affected. For this calculation, population totals are needed. For example, if those same 4,000 burglaries occurred within a community of 250,000 people, then 1,600 out of every 100,000 people, or about 1 out of every 63 people, are being burglarized (Remember, the rate per 100,000 people is the figure being sought). Then 250,000 equals 2 · 5 times 100,000, therefore 4,000 (burglaries)/2 · 5 (100,000 people) = 1,600 burglaries per 100,000 people. If it's to be determined, roughly, how many people are affected out of each 100,000, divide 100,000 by 1,600. Thus it is ascertained that 1 out of every 63 people are affected.

This may be taken further if desired. Assume an average of 4 people per family, then 1 out of every 16 families are personally affected (63 ÷ 4 = 16, approximately). Similar calculations with data obtained from another jurisdiction will provide a comparison. Some planners prefer to use a rate per 1,000, in which case (in the initial calculation) divide by 250 instead of 2 · 5 (250 × 100 = 250,000). It may still be determined that 1 out of every 63 people are affected, and similarly, 1 out of every 16 families.

By comparing figures with some other jurisdiction (i.e., city, county, state), it can be determined whether this particular jurisdiction is significantly higher or lower, thereby giving a seriousness factor relative to that experienced in other areas.

Location

Location simply means where the problem is occurring. The planner should know these general boundaries. It could be, for example, that the problem is so general that all the planner can say is that it is countywide. Perhaps, though, one city out of five in the county has the problem to a greater degree. Determining the problem by degree or determining where it is the worst does not lessen the problem in the other areas. It just gives the planner one more piece of information in terms of problem identification.

Who

Generally speaking, who is committing the crime? Arrest reports will give some explanation. From a statistical point of view one must ask; is the problem caused by adult, juvenile, male, or female offenders? Further information can be obtained describing social, educational, and economic background. In addition to statistical analysis, two other techniques can be used to corroborate findings. One is the Delphi analysis, and the other is Attitude survey.

Delphi

Planning must take into account both the actual and perceived. That is, what is true and what people believe to be true. In addition to the analysis of data that essentially reflects what is actually occurring, there is a definite need to question those who are involved with the criminal justice system (i.e., police, lawyers, judges, probation, corrections, criminals). The attitudes and relationship among the disassociated segments of the system and the elected officials with whom they relate are critical to the performance of planning objectives and programs, and any long-term reform. The key to the success of any plan is the total involvement of these individuals (from problem identification to assessment of priorities). One thing to remember is, if key personnel are not in the plan's development, they can be expected to be equally aloof regarding its implementation.

The essence of the Delphi technique is the ability to first solicit unheard individual opinions on a given issue and then share these personal responses with the total group. This allows additional input and individual reevaluation. As the process continues, one or more ideas emerge that address the problem. A detailed analysis of the Delphi technique is presented in Chapter IV.

Attitude Survey

Equally important (for meaningful input into the problem identification process) is assistance from the community at large. While it is true that most members of society lack an acute understanding of the details of the criminal justice system, they *do* know what bothers them. The community can also provide information relating to what programs they would like to see increased and conversely, which programs might be reduced or eliminated. Their perceptions of problems, whether general or more specific, relating to crime need to be compared with those ideas perceived through the Delphi analysis. In addition, community perception of crime problems can be compared with the problems identified through statistical analysis.

Finally, the planner can determine the relationship the various problem areas have with one another. This is a useful tool when establishing goals, objectives, and priorities in the planning process. To accomplish this, a matrix can be prepared utilizing the information obtained for each problem area based upon the problem parameters, Delphi analysis and Attitude survey. Of the five parameters, magnitude, rate of change, and seriousness become a part of the matrix. The problem areas are ranked in order of priority, number one being the highest priority, based on the criteria for each parameter. Similarly, problem areas are ranked according to the results of both the Delphi analysis, and Attitude survey. The summation of the matrix gives the planner an idea of the most pressing problem, plus the relative relationship of other problem areas. Figure III-5 gives an example of a matrix used in this fashion. In the example, Problem A, of the problems studied, would receive first priority, because the matrix total for Problem A is the least. The second priority would be assigned to Problem C, followed by Problems B and D.

PROBLEM / CRITERIA	PROBLEM A	PROBLEM B	PROBLEM C	PROBLEM D
MAGNITUDE	1	3	2	4
SERIOUSNESS	3	1	4	2
RATE OF CHANGE	2	4	3	1
DELPHI SURVEY	1	3	2	4
ATTITUDE SURVEY	4	2	1	3
TOTALS EACH ROW	11	13	12	14

Figure III-5. Problem priority matrix.

ESTABLISHING GOALS AND OBJECTIVES

Once a problem has been identified, and the decision has been made to resolve it, it is important to next develop it in perspective. In terms of a system problem, for example, is it the intended purpose to try to solve the whole thing or a part of it? Is the attempt to reduce crime or keep it from increasing too fast? Will only specific crime areas be examined? If so, the same question can be asked. And, of course, what is to be the proposed course of action?

Planners usually attempt to derive an agency mission statement and identify goals or objectives by reviewing the original legislative intent. This can be accomplished by reading documents, e.g., the statute and legislative records or debates. In addition, officials can be interviewed (legislators, legislative staff, budget analysts, and program administrators). One can also consult with those outside the government who have an interest or stake in the programs operation, e.g., recipients, lobbyists, dissatisfied groups, or advocacy groups.

In many instances, such research results in the identification of vague statements of intent or conflicting interpretations. Jerome T. Murphy has suggested that it might be preferable to look at the program in the light of its current goals developed through experience in actual program implementation (Murphy, 1980).

Many agencies start with a very broad mission statement that provides generalized direction for the agency. Typical of this is a police agency where the mission statement focuses on crime control, order maintenance, service delivery, and traffic management (National Institute of Justice, 1982). The mission categories can be utilized to analyze the relationship of problem categories to conventional definitions of a police agency mission statement. (See Figure III-6).

Category	Definition	Percent of Calls
1. CRIME CONTROL MISSION	Violent crimes, nonviolent crimes, public morals crime, suspicious circumstances, warrants and officer assists.	36%
2. ORDER MAINTENANCE MISSION	Interpersonal conflicts, disturbances, nuisances, dependent persons if the crime category does not apply and any one of these categories does apply then the problem or event reported to police is in the order maintenance category.	22%
3. SERVICE DELIVERY MISSION	Assistance, information, request, information for police. If neither the crime nor the order maintenance categories apply and one of these categories does, then the incident is in the service category.	30%
4. TRAFFIC MANAGEMENT MISSION	Traffic problems. If neither crime nor order maintenance nor service delivery categories apply to the incident and the traffic problem category does, then it is considered in the traffic category.	12%

Figure III-6. Relationship of categories to general police missions.

The establishment and accomplishment of goals and objectives follow such similar paths that the words *goal* and *objective* are often interchanged. Authorities generally agree that *goal* is a more general term than *objective*.

Goal—A statement of broad direction, general purpose, or intent. A goal is general and timeless and is not concerned with a particular achievement within a specified time period.

Objective—A desired accomplishment that can be measured within a given time frame and under specific conditions. The attainment of the objective advances the system toward a corresponding goal.

Fundamental to the establishment of all goals and objectives is a perception of the problems encountered or anticipated by the agency. Clear definition and careful analysis of the factors generating the problem may clearly indicate possible solutions and suggest appropriate goals and objectives. On the other hand, the failure to perceive or to understand a problem may lead to the establishment of goals or objectives that could be nonproductive or even counterproductive (National Advisory Commission on Criminal Justice Standards and Goals, 1973).

It is our objective to critically analyse and develop a sense of importance on how goals and objectives contribute to the planning process. The agencies making up the criminal justice system have traditionally lacked the understanding of formulating goals, to provide a framework for that agency to assess its effectiveness. This chapter will possibly provide insight into the process and the effect it has on the system of criminal justice.

GOALS

Etzioni (1946) states that "the goals of organizations serve many functions. They provide orientation by depicting a future state of affairs which the organization strives to realize." He further clarifies goals by stating the following:

> Goals constitute a source of legitimacy which justify the activities of the organization. Goals serve as standards by which members of an organization and outsiders assess the success of the organization (effectiveness and efficiency).

The importance of goal formulation as an integral part of the planning process is vital. The goal articulation defines the desired state of affairs that one is striving to achieve. Without the articulation of goals, planning becomes futile. One is left without the mission direction needed to develop and measure plans. This problem has plagued the criminal justice system and its agencies.

As an illustration of goals, the reader may review the *goals of corrections.* Anyone familiar with the history of corrections in the United States knows that a wide range of goals has evolved as practitioners, academicians, policymakers, and other interested parties have struggled with what it is that corrections should be doing. The result has been that many goals have been articulated and conflicting goals can be found within a single state and even within a single correctional program. The following is a typical list of goals for corrections that can be found in the literature. These goals collectively reflect the conflicts that have developed. It is necessary to be able to link program activities with goals, and a subset of the following goals will be of benefit in a particular application:

Revenge, in modern interpretation, is the retaliation of the state through incarceration, capital punishment, or some other form of payment by the individual to the society for transgressions.

Restraint may be defined as restricting the individual's freedom of activity. It may range from placing an offender in a small, narrow solitary confinement cell to requiring an offender to report once a month to a probation or parole officer. Probation and parole conditions place limits on the activities of persons under their auspices.

Punishment is defined as taking some set of the freedoms from the individual, such as incarcerating an offender to remove him from society or requiring the offender to report to a community-based facility, or a probation or parole officer. Note that revenge, restraint, and punishment are overlapping concepts with no clear-cut distinctions.

Protection of society includes activities for preventing crime and reducing the fear of crime. Prisons, for example, protect society by keeping offenders from committing further criminal acts.

Enhancing justice, for correctional agencies, has to do with bringing about the sentences that have been imposed by the courts or, in the case of diversion, the decisions that have been made by other parts of the criminal justice system.

Restitution is the offender's paying society or the victim an amount offsetting the loss incurred by the offender's criminal action. The payment may be in the form of financial compensation or work or service to the community.

Reform changes the emphasis from revenge and restraint to treatment and rehabilitation. Correctional programs have reform aspects by providing counseling, education opportunities, and employment assistance.

Reintegration seeks to bring about change in the offender and to stimulate outside community aid to support the individual in moving away from criminal behavior (Grizzle, 1980).

GOAL-SETTING PROCESS

In the context of the criminal justice system, goals are viewed as a desired state of affairs for the system. One recent article indicates that (Leach, 1974) *the overall goal and purpose of the criminal justice system is the elimination of crime and delinquency.* The author further qualifies this by contending that this statement of purpose seems obvious; however, many persons within the system do not function in relation to it.

Some judges just try cases. Some district attorneys just prosecute. Some police just catch offenders. Officials who so limit their roles indicate that they do not function in relation to the purpose of the system. Their goal is some subordinate part of the production line. They revere a bush or a rock rather than the universe (Leach, 1974). Perhaps this view leads to taking a systematic look at the criminal justice system, realizing that system components (police, courts, etc.) have an impact upon each other. If this is the case, the need to articulate criminal justice goals would seem obvious. The political subdivision of counties would appear the logical starting point for goal articulation, since each county has a representative criminal justice system. That is, all the components are operating at the county level. The goal setting could be done by a working board made up of representative heads of the agencies. To be effective, such goal setting would require executive level participation. The results might read as follows in a particular county:

1. Eliminate inappropriate use of criminal sanctions.
   a. develop new remedies for victimless crimes
2. Reduce the processing time of offenders in the system.
   a. develop alternatives to arrest
   b. develop common sense *speedy* trial and appeal procedures

Once a specific crime problem has been identified, there are two basic responses: *reduce the cause* of the problem and improve control of the problem. *Cause* is reduced either by attacking underlying social, economic, or other basic conditions that promote the commission of crime. Obviously, much program activity in this regard is outside the authority and responsibility of the criminal justice system. Nonetheless, social, demographic, and other economic data related to crime analysis can point to obvious areas of interagency or intergovernmental cooperation of benefit to the community in areas beyond that simply of crime control. On another level, *cause* can be reduced by intervening in criminal careers through programs involving identified offender groups or through what frequently are called *prevention* programs, such as youth service bureaus or school attendance projects in high juvenile crime areas.

Control is improved either by reducing opportunity for the commission of criminal acts or by increasing the risks of offending. Examples of the former include target-hardening activities such as physical security improvement or property identification. Examples of the latter include concentrated police patrol and the speedy adjudication of target crime cases.

Crime-oriented planning, therefore, leads to the establishment of comprehensive program goals that involve the whole system of criminal justice. It is not simply a police suppression model.

Goals should be hierarchical and quantitative. There may be initial resistance by operating agency personnel to the establishment of quantitative goals. However, quantitative goals provide for clarity of purpose and the measurement of program/project results. They are an integral component of crime-oriented planning.

In hierarchical terms, at the state level, a major program goal might be the reduction of burglary by 5 percent within one year in the five largest metropolitan areas. At the city level, this goal might translate to a reduction of residential burglaries by 10 percent and a reduction of commercial burglaries by 5 percent.

The selection and development of projects continues this process of quantification. *Tactical alternatives* to meet state or city goals must be weighed and chosen. What type or types of program activities respond most directly and effectively to identified problems and established goals? The utility of data collection and problem analysis is severely hindered if the full examination of alternatives is shortchanged, or if data are collected and molded solely to justify the selection of a predetermined project activity.

The process of alternative selection takes place through a screen of real world *constraints* that can be political, legal, economic, social, moral, or ethical in nature. Highly competent planners and a sophisticated rational supervisory board might agree that a particular alternative offers the best possibility for reducing the target crime, yet they may not select that alternative for implementation because it is economically unfeasible, patently illegal, or otherwise contrary to prevailing community standards. Constraints are natural and they must be understood by planners; the difficulty arises in not letting the possibility of constraints that may be imposed unduly hinder the planner in the full development and examination of alternate tactics and programs.

The selection from among alternatives yields a plan of related program activities that can span the criminal justice system and include some activities even outside the system. Selected activities can include programs related to the prevention of the target crime; the detection, deterrence, and apprehension of offenders, the diversion of offenders from the criminal justice system, the adjudication of offenders, and the rehabilitation of offenders, through both institutional and noninstitutional programs. Data collection and analysis also may point out the need for legislative change, additional data and information systems, or additional research, all of which frequently are overlooked in the search for alternative courses of action.

Based upon choices from among alternatives, we can imagine the following project activities and goals developed in accordance with the *reduce cause–improve control* approach to a city-level burglary reduction goal:

1. A property identification project to enroll **X** persons and mark **Y** amount of property within the census tracts with highest burglary rates.
2. A concentrated crime patrol aimed at providing **X** amount of patrol and **Y** response time during peak hours in the high burglary census tracts, increasing by **Z** the amount of burglary arrests.

3. A reduction in court backlog for burglary cases by **X**, and an increase in burglary convictions by **Y**, through the addition of judicial and prosecutorial personnel.
4. Offender-based programs for burglary offenders such as drug diversion (where offender drug abuse is substantial) or juvenile diversion projects (where juveniles are found to constitute a substantial percentage of burglary offenders).

Several comments can be made about these project examples. First, many of the particular activities undertaken as a response to crime-oriented problem analysis are not necessarily different or unique from those that are undertaken where reliance on data is less extensive. The difference is that these activities are undertaken in response to specifically identified and bounded problems and their goals and operation, location, and scope of services or products are carefully related to the magnitude and nature of the problem. Second, products or results (effectiveness objectives) and levels of service (efficiency objectives) are clearly specified, providing for clarity of purpose and the evaluation of results and performance (Payne, 1975).

OBJECTIVES

Objectives are different from goals. They are more specific and are measurable against a dimension of time. For example, the goal to reduce processing time of offenders would have to be qualified with objectives. An illustration might read as follows:

To reduce the criminal justice processing time of offenders by ten days within the next fiscal year.

This objective is measurable and has a specific time frame for accomplishment. The objectives provide a basis for looking at and brainstorming solutions or programs to meet the specific objective and thus achieving the goal.

The writing of objectives should meet the following criteria (City of Palo Alto, 1973):

1. An objective must be stated in terms of results, not process or activities.
2. The results of an objective must be specific, not general, and must be recognizable and understandable so it will be recognized when objectives have been met.
3. An objective must be measurable. The evaluation criteria should be built into the objective statement. This implies that the objective will be quantifiable.
4. An objective must be achievable and feasible within specific time frames.

5. An objective should be oriented to some audience or user of service.

Objectives that can meet the preceding criteria provide a viable base for program procedures that will allow for the measurement of the program of an agency or division toward satisfying its objectives (City of Palo Alto, 1973).

There should be a definite link between the broad goal and specific objectives, as this serves as a foundation for evaluation. The need to establish the goal/objective relationship is vital.

The emphasis for criminal justice agencies to assess productivity and to be accountable for performance will present ever-increasing challenges. The beginning step is to develop a planning capability that can serve as the vehicle to assess productivity toward stated goals and objectives.

PITFALLS IN PLANNING

Up to this point many of the positive attributes of planning have been discussed, but some of the pitfalls that planners fall into as they go through their planning process have been overlooked. The remainder of this chapter will be dedicated to a brief description of potential planning problem areas.

Gathering Excessive Data

As planners begin to perform their job, they typically become obsessed with the need for more data. They tend to look at data in terms of absoluteness, that is, they are looking to describe something from data in a finite form. Actually, the converse is true; data should be used as an indicator of change or rate of change. We are not so concerned that a given jurisdiction had twenty-five homicides as we are with knowing whether homicides are increasing or decreasing and at what rate.

The planner should select in advance the minimal data needed to make a decision with 70 to 80 percent certainty. The planner must select data sources carefully in order to identify the most useful and pertinent. A good rule of thumb to consider is that 80 to 90 percent of planning can be accomplished with data that is readily available, thus requiring only 10 percent of the planning resources to assimilate. In order to get the remaining 10 to 20 percent will require an investment of almost 90 percent of your planning resources. Capturing original data is a time-consuming and expensive proposition and should be considered only after all other readily available sources of data have been explored.

Misinterpretation of Data

In reviewing and analyzing data, keep the problem in mind and be sure that the data applies. It is so easy to "lose sight of the forest because of the trees." If uncertainty arises as to the meaningfulness of the data, do not be afraid to seek the opinion and judgment of others who are knowledgeable. Agency heads or supervisors are a great help in interpreting data once it has been separated into a digestible format.

Inadequate Definition of the Problem

As the planner defines the problem, the limits or boundaries of the problem description must also be defined. By doing this, the planner will set a finite number of factors influencing the problem that can reasonably be addressed. If the boundaries are not defined, a chain reaction of seemingly endless problem area influences will occur. As one influence is identified, factors impeding the influence will be discovered until the planner will become so lost in the trivia of cause and effect that one could forget or lose sight of the initial problem. Again, advice from appropriate and knowledgeable criminal justice agency personnel can be an asset in establishing problem area boundaries.

Lack of Understanding of the Criminal Justice System

The planner tends to oversimplify the workings of the criminal justice system. One reason—an incomplete awareness of the day-to-day operations, procedures, technicalities, and internal influences of the system. This calls for recognizing this handicap and seeking input from people and literature that expresses these problem and solution impeding influences.

Establishment of Irrelevant Objectives

As was stated earlier, all objectives should be quantified and bound by a time constraint. Additionally, they must be related to the accomplishment of a specific goal. All objectives tend to get compromised as policymakers realize that they are committing themselves to a specific output over a given time. In order to protect the goal maker from potential failure, they will represent a constant challenge to planners and evaluators for many years to come.

Premature Acceptance of a Plan Without Considering Alternatives

As long as criminal justice planning is tied to the chariot of federal funding, the planner is going to be placed in the position of finding problems to fit desired solutions. The planner must make an effort to expose policy people to the fact that more than one solution approach is possible and that sufficient regard should be given to the feasibility consideration discussed in a previous chapter.

Improper Allocation to Solution Resources

The planning process spends considerable time in the prioritization of problems, goals, and solutions only to find that resources to solve the problem are distributed haphazardly between high– and low-priority areas. Work on the most critical problems first. Allocate resources in proportion to the importance of the problem, giving proper attention to the most critical. Policymakers are encouraged to allocate sufficient funds to each project to assure that stated objectives will be attained.

Lack of Criteria for Appraisal

Solution-oriented projects and tasks should be monitored frequently based upon performance standards for appraising progress. The whole purpose of this is not to penalize someone for doing a poor job, but rather to take timely corrective action when needed.

Insufficient Emphasis on Planning Organization

As a planning activity begins to take hold in an organization, the planning unit becomes saddled with a multitude of duties and activities simply because it has available manpower and no one else seems to be appropriate for the job. Many times this is a result of the planner wanting to be accepted in an organization, so the planning group deals with almost any request that is funneled in its direction. This is a good idea during the formation period of the planning group. It helps them integrate into the organization. However, the planner must be aware of a primary mission, and that is planning. It is imperative to focus efforts on planning and minimize other duties, also being cautious to assign or assume planning responsibilities in proportion to staff size and workload.

Lack of Coordination with Other Activities

One of the major activities of planning is coordination. If the planner does not coordinate, nobody else will. The planner should identify the universe of problems related to certain efforts at state, regional, local, and departmental levels. After ascertaining relationships with other agency efforts, a working relationship with the planning staffs of these organizational units can be established.

These are but a few of the pitfalls that will confront a planner during operations on a daily basis. Obviously, many more problems will be encountered. The key to success is to not loose sight of the planning objective, even if this means compromising a smaller portion of it to gain the greater share (O'Neill, 1976).

This chapter has attempted to point out a process through which a planner should approach problem analysis. It focuses on need determination, problem analysis, and the establishing of goals and objectives. In the next chapter, consideration is given to a review of planning techniques.

TOPICS FOR DISCUSSION

1. Why is it important to first determine a need?
2. Why is it important for the planner to develop good idea sources?
3. What is the significance behind an understanding of causative relationship?
4. What is the process involved with problem identification?
5. Differentiate between a goal and an objective.
6. Identify the elements of a causitive relationship.
7. Describe a typical problem statement.
8. Differentiate between magnitude and rate of change.

REFERENCES

Albanese, Robert. *Management: Toward Accountability for Performance.* Richard D. Auchincloss, Publisher, 1975.

Beck, Arthur C., Jr., and Hillmar, Ellis D. *Making MBO/R Work.* Reading, Massachusetts: Addison-Wesley Publishing Co., 1976.

City of Palo Alto. *Municipal Service Handbook.* Palo Alto, California, 1973.

Etzioni, Amitai. *Modern Organizations.* New York: Prentice-Hall, 1964.

Franklin, Billy J., and Osborne, Harold A. *Research Methods: Issues and Insights.* Belmont, California: Wadsworth Publishing Co., 1971.

Gottfredson, Don M. *Decision Making in the Criminal Justice System: Review and Essays.* Rockville, Maryland: National Institute of Mental Health, 1975.

Grizzle, Gloria A. *Measuring Corrections Performance.* Raleigh, North Carolina: The Osprey Company, 1980.

Isaac, Stephen. *Handbook in Research and Evaluation*. San Diego, CA: Robert R. Knapp, Publisher, 1974.

LEAA. *Planning and Designing for Juvenile Justice*. Washington: U.S. Government Printing Office, August, 1972.

Leach, Edmund. A plan for meaningful justice. *Crime Prevention Review*, October, 1974.

Lereton, Preston, and Henning, Dale. *Planning Theory*. New Jersey: Prentice-Hall, 1961.

MITRE Corporation. *Evaluation in Criminal Justice Programs: Guidelines and Examples*. Washington, D.C.: Law Enforcement Assistance Administration, National Institute of Law Enforcement and Criminal Justice, May, 1973.

More, Harry W. Jr., editor. *Effective Police Administration*, 2nd Edition. St. Paul, Minnesota: West Publishing, 1979.

Murphy, Jerome T. *Getting the Facts*. Santa Monica, California: Goodyear Publishing Co., 1980.

National Advisory Commission on Criminal Justice Standards and Goals. *Police*. Washington, D.C.: G.P.O., 1973.

Selltiz, Claire, Johoda, Marie, Deutsch, Morton, and Cook, Stuart W. *Research Methods in Social Relations*. New York: Holt, Rinehart and Winston, 1959.

Whitaker, Gordon P., Mastrofski, Stephen, Ostrom, Elinor, Parks, Roger B., and Percy, Stephen L. *Measuring Police Agency Performance*. Washington D.C.: National Institute of Justice, 1980.

Chapter IV

PLANNING TECHNIQUES

Several techniques are discussed in this chapter that can be categorized under the three methods of data collection discussed previously. These techniques are partially inclusive, and one or more can be utilized in the same study. The nature of the data collected will, in some instances, proscribe the technique that will be utilized. In other cases, this is not true. For example, descriptive analysis is not limited to any one method of data collection, while Delphi is limited to field data collection.

The techniques set forth in this chapter are those that have been used most often in studying criminal justice (see Table IV-1).

Table IV-1
PLANNING TECHNIQUES

Baseline Data
  Descriptive Analysis
  Content Analysis
  Statistical Analysis
    Frequency Distribution
    Measures of Central Tendency
      Mean
      Median
      Mode
    Univariate Statistics
    Multivariate Statistics
Field Data
  Delphi
  Delbecq
  Roundtable
  Magnitude Estimation
  Case Study
Experimental Data
  Structured Experiences
  Modeling
  Models
  Simulations
  PERT/CPM
  Queuing Theory

BASELINE DATA COLLECTION TECHNIQUES

The selection of one of the following techniques is conditioned by the specific research problem, the research questions postulated by the investigator, and the limitations of the specific technique.

The techniques that are especially useful are the following:

1. Descriptive analysis
2. Content analysis
3. Statistical analysis

The application of one of these scientific techniques increases the likelihood that the information gathered will be relevant to the questions asked and compatible with the research design discussed in the previous chapter.

Descriptive Analysis

Descriptive analysis is a technique utilized when portraying an event or activity, a problem, etc. that has occurred.

The procedures used in a descriptive study must be carefully planned (Selltiz, 1959). In an effort to obtain complete and accurate information, the research design must consider such factors as the potentiality of researcher bias and the concern for economy of research effort.

The objectives of the study normally provide a framework for description. For example, suppose we want a descriptive analysis of patrol workload in a community. The key question is, What does the officer do on patrol? Previous research in this area indicates that patrol activity can be divided into the following four basic functional categories

1. Calls for service
2. Preventive patrol
3. Officer-initiated activities
4. Administrative tasks

Each category is described in detail. The researcher, however, does not endeavor to explain relationships or test a hypothesis. Note that the criminal justice planner does not introduce any judgmental characteristics into the report, but merely describes how the program is functioning based on the analysis of the categories.

The purpose of descriptive research (Isaac, 1974) is to

1. collect detailed factual information
2. identify problems or justify current conditions and practices
3. make comparisons and evaluations
4. determine what other planners are doing with similar problems

The specific steps in descriptive analysis include

1. defining the objectives in clear, specific terms
2. designing the approach
3. collecting the data
4. reporting the results

An enormous number of descriptive studies have been conducted describing or summarizing survey research proceeding under the auspices of the federal government. Typical of these are the Prescriptive Packages (National Institute of Law Enforcement and Criminal Justice, 1978) that are listed in Table IV-2.

Table IV-2
PRESCRIPTIVE PACKAGES

Child Abuse Intervention
Crime Scene Search and Physical Evidence Handbook
Drug Programs in Correctional Institutions
Evaluation Research in Corrections
Grievance Mechanisms in Correctional Institutions
Guide to Improved Handling of Misdemeanant Offenders
Improving Patrol Productivity, Vol. 1—Routine Patrol
Improving Patrol Productivity, Vol. 2—Specialized Patrol
Improving Police-Community Relations
Managing Criminal Investigations
MBO: A Corrections Perspective
Multi-Agency Narcotics Units Manual
Neighborhood Team Policing
Police Crime Analysis Units
Police Robbery Control Manual
Prosecutor's Charging Decision
Rape and Its Victims
Volunteers in Juvenile Justice

Content Analysis

Content analysis is a research technique for making replicative and valid inferences from data (Krippendorff, 1980). It seeks to understand data not as a collection of physical events, but as symbolic phenomena. The task is to make inferences from data to specific aspects of their content and then to justify these inferences in terms of one's knowledge about the stable factors inherent in the system being studied.

A conceptual framework for content analysis includes the following basic elements (Krippendorff, 1980):

1. The data as collected by the researcher
2. The context of the data

3. The target of the study
4. Inference as the basic intellectual tool
5. Validity as the criteria of success

From one point of view, it is reasonable to call content analysis a *qualitative* technique, for the planner does not make quantitative comparisons between two or more cases (Simon, 1969).

A planner may say that one police agency is *more law enforcement oriented* than another, but such a statement cannot be substantiated numerically. If you ask the planner to prove his statement quantitatively, he may reply that you are asking him to measure the unmeasurable. But content analysis is actually a method of measuring the unmeasurable—at least to some extent—and from this point of view it is sensible to call it a *quantitative* technique.

The content analysis planner sets up various classification schemes, then applies them to speeches, writings, or other data. These classifications either count specific kinds of words or ideas, or they measure the amount of words or time devoted to particular ideas. An example might consist of looking for key words in departmental general orders, providing a clue to that department's philosophy.

Content analysis can be used in studies of the mass media to determine changes in either the media or in society's perception of criminal justice. It is a formalization of techniques that have long been used informally. For example, a planner may count the number of favorable or unfavorable editorials in a county's newspaper to see how the climate toward criminal justice has changed from one period to the next, rather than merely obtaining an informal impression of the climate.

Statistical Analysis

This is probably the most widely used technique in criminal justice baseline data manipulation. The publication by the National Advisory Commission on Criminal Justice Standards and Goals (Criminal Justice System, 1973) discussed statistical analysis by stating the following:

> Methods and techniques of statistical analysis provide avenues to study and precisely describe data—its relationships, differences, and distribution. The major aim of statistics is to compare actual results with chance expectations toward the end of reducing uncertainty in decision-making. Toward this goal it treats all empirical data as chance happenings until shown to be otherwise.

In order to enhance our understanding of basic statistics, those most commonly used and their application are described below.

Frequency Distribution

A frequency distribution displays a pattern of scores or numbers. For example, let's say you have just surveyed the community concerning its attitude toward the police. You developed a score for each question, giving you possible scores from 0 to 15. The first step in frequency distribution is to find the highest and lowest scores. Then arrange the other scores in descending order. This simple frequency distribution is set forth in Table IV-3. The scores are listed in simple rank order, from highest to lowest, in column one and the frequencies in column two.

Table IV-3
SIMPLE FREQUENCY DISTRIBUTION

Score	Frequency
15	2
14	9
13	28
12	90
11	110
10	70
9	63
8	31
7	15
6	8
5	3
	N = 329

Frequency is merely a descriptive statistic telling how many times a given score occurs in data collection. These frequencies could then be depicted by a bar graph in order to facilitate interpretation. Figure IV-1 depicts the frequency distribution as a histogram. In this instance, the scores are plotted along the horizontal baseline (abscissa), and the frequencies are plotted along the vertical axis (ordinate). The height of each bar represents the number of cases for each score.

Measures of Central Tendency

One statistic often used in looking at criminal justice data is the measures of central tendency. These are the mean, mode, and median—the most frequently employed measures—and are best described as an index of central location employed in the description of frequency distributions (Runyon and Haber, 1968).

The measures of central tendency permit the criminal justice planner to make quantitative statements either describing the distribution or comparing two or more distributions.

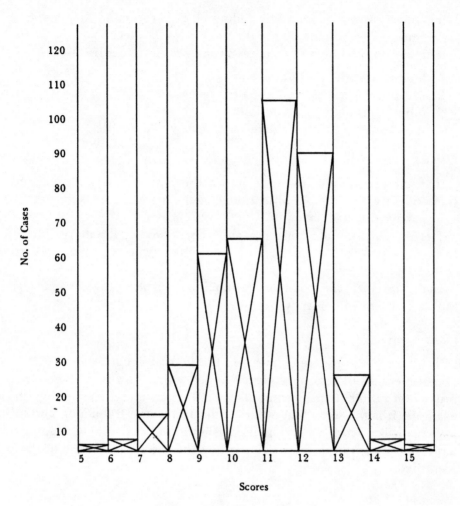

Figure IV-1. Histogram.

Mean

The mean is found by dividing the sum of a series of scores (measures) by the number of scores made. An example is a supervisory promotional exam is given to seven patrolmen, and their scores were the following:

Sample	Test Score
Patrolman 1	50
Patrolman 2	60
Patrolman 3	80
Patrolman 4	90
Patrolman 5	100
Patrolman 6	90
Patrolman 7	10

The mean would be found by adding all the scores and then dividing by the number of patrolmen taking the test ($480 \div 7 = 68.5$).

The mean is computed by the researcher when (Isaac, 1974)—

1. the greatest reliability is wanted;
2. the distribution is approximately normal;
3. other computations are to follow;
4. it is desirable to know the *center of gravity* of a sample.

Median

The median divides the area under the curve into two equal halves. Consequently, the number of scores below the median equals the number of scores above the median.

It is especially useful when scores are badly skewed. In the above illustration, the median promotional exam score is 80. This is true even with the extreme score of 10.

In this instance, the mean promotional score of 68.5 provides a misleading estimate of central tendency.

Mode

The mode is the score or measure that most frequently occurs. It is the easiest measure of central tendency to determine because it is obtained by inspection rather than by computation (Runyon and Haber, 1978). In our example, it is the score that occurs with the greatest frequency, and in this instance it is a score of 90. The mode should only be used when a planner desires a quick, rough estimate, or when the most typical case needs to be identified.

Univariate Statistics

Consider the issue of delay in the time it takes for the court to process cases. We can describe this phenomenon in the absence of any other factor using *univariate* statistics. Univariate statistics are useful in providing measures that describe the way that cases are distributed over the time it takes the court to process them. Figure IV-2 depicts such a distribution.

As with most pictures, Figure IV-2 describes case processing time better, perhaps, than would a thousand words that only characterize the picture. It is, nonetheless, convenient to be able to describe the distribution of case processing time in terms of certain statistical measures. One might say, for example, that more cases leave the system on the first day than on any other day—more briefly, that the *mode* is one day; or that half the cases are processed within the first 45 days—more briefly, that the *median* is 45 days; or

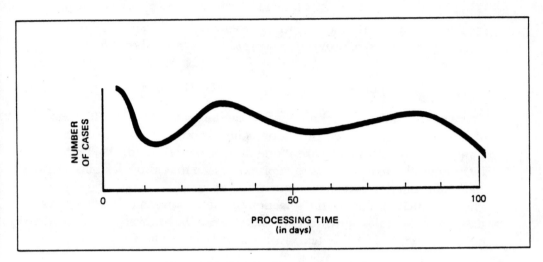

Figure IV-2. Distribution of cases over time.

that the *mean* (i.e., average) number of days to process a case is 50; or that the distribution is *polymodal*, with peaks at days one (due to rejections of cases at screening), 30 (the mode number of days to misdemeanor trials), and 80 (the mode number of days to felony trials); or that the *range*, a measure of the total dispersion or spread of the distribution, is 150 days.

Such measures are useful for making definitive quantitative comparisons of case processing times in one jurisdiction with those in another. These statistics also serve as important components of multivariate analysis.

Multivariate Statistics

Of more policy relevance than the univariate characteristics of case processing time are the multivariate relationships between case processing time and other factors. For example, if the mean case processing time for felony cases increased from 70 to 100 days, what would happen to the percentage of cases that go to trial? Or, if witnesses were paid a sum of money to appear in court so that continuances were reduced to, say, 30 percent, what would happen to the mean case processing time? We can see that it is useful to know both how case processing time affects other factors (e.g., witness cooperativeness, convictions, and recidivism), and what factors influence case processing time (e.g., experience of the prosecutor, defense counsel, and judge; existence of tangible evidence; and degree to which the defendant is a *career criminal*). In the former case, we would be looking at case processing time as a cause. In the latter case, we would be looking at case processing time as an effect. Such issues as these can be addressed using tools of multivariate statistical analysis (Forst, 1975).

For a further in-depth understanding of statistical analysis and the type of statistics, an annotated bibliography is provided at the end of this chapter.

FIELD DATA COLLECTION TECHNIQUES

There are a number of techniques that can be grouped under the term of field data collection. This classification is not a mutually exclusive scheme, and there is no intention to make it one-dimensional (Simon, 1969).

Techniques discussed in this category are those that allow for qualitative methods of deduction rather than quantitative.

There is much overlap in the selection of a technique that can be applied to data. For example, statistical techniques can be utilized in all of the techniques discussed in this text. In addition, one could argue that a case study is almost synonymous with descriptive analysis. The key is that the discussion framework utilized has been created as a vehicle to aid understanding (not hinder it).

This section of the chapter discusses the following techniques:

1. Delphi
2. Delbecq
3. Roundtable
4. Magnitude Estimation
5. Case Study

These techniques are primarily the qualitative type, allowing human judgment to fill informational needs. Consequently, whenever possible, they should be used with quantitative findings.

Delphi

The Delphi technique allows a number of individuals to communicate with each other anonymously regarding a complex problem. It is a positive system for facilitating the analysis of solutions and the development of decision options. It is a quasi-empirical forecasting technique developed by the Rand Corporation of California and deals with unknown quantities or factors such as future events. It is a means of arriving at working conclusions regarding a specific subject matter through the use of expert knowledge.

Individuals are chosen for inclusion on a Delphi panel by virtue of their knowledge, experience, and ability to project decision options based upon that knowledge and experience; hence, they are classified as experts. Individual participants are interrogated by a sequence of questionnaires in which the responses to one questionnaire is designed and structured around a particular topic.

The resulting environment of the Delphi method is a communication process (as opposed to a poll), since individuals have the opportunity to change their earlier views and to benefit from the contributions of others. A clear-cut advantage is that the process eliminates psychological factor-bias. (Gordon and Helmer, 1964).

With the first questionnaire each panel member is required to give the best estimate of the answer to each question. The questionnaire can, of course, contain any number of questions pertaining to a variety of subjects if they come within the realm of the members' expertise.

When the questionnaires are received from the panel members, each question is tabulated by the researcher to determine the median and range of the interquartile for each question. This is done upon the receipt of each round of questionnaires.

The second questionnaire is then prepared. It contains the original questions and entries to show the new medians and interquartile ranges. Each member is then asked to review the first estimate and change it, if they are so inclined.

The panel member is now instructed that if his answer at this time is still outside the range of the interquartile, he should present substantiating information.

The third questionnaire is then prepared. It contains the original questions and a newly computed median and interquartile range. A summary of all comments made by the panel members on the second questionnaire is included.

Each panel member now reviews all information given and adjusts their answer to each question if they alter their position. Each panel member whose answer now is within the interquartile range is requested to provide comments as to why the additional information received did not sway them to move their answer to one of the relatively extreme positions.

When the researcher receives all of the completed third questionnaires, a fourth one is prepared, if it is necessary. It will contain the original questions, a newly computed median and interquartile range, and a summary of all the comments submitted on the second and third questionnaires. Each panel member now has all the information developed in the study and is requested to make a final review of all the information and to determine a final answer to each question. All completed questionnaires are then returned to the researcher. (Morrow, 1972).

One recent use of this technique was utilized in forecasting criminalistics goals and requirements (Illinois Law Enforcement Commission, 1975):

In this case a group of eight expert panelists were put through a series of rounds to

forecast future 10-year criminalistic goals. They were then put through another series
of rounds to forecast future requirements based upon five criteria:

1. Organizational structure.
2. Service demands.
3. Manpower needs.
4. Needed support system.
5. Delivery of service.

Another Delphi study conducted by one of the coauthors forecast the
control of police corruption.

A panel of police officials and police educators responded to the following
three open-ended questions:

1. What have been the significant trends concerning the extent and nature of police corruption and its control during the last ten years?
2. During the next twenty-five years, do you anticipate these trends to
   continue in the same direction and at the same rates, or do you
   anticipate significant changes? Please explain.
3. Do you forsee any new trends in the control of police corruption
   emerging during the next twenty-five years? Please explain.

Upon completion of the study, the panel of experts suggested that during
the next twenty-five years, police professionalization would emerge as the
most important factor in the control of police corruption. Of the data items,
33 percent dealt specifically with the concept of police professionalization;
38 percent of the items positively supported the concept of professionalization
and served to reinforce and amplify the significance of this trend as well as to
establish the interrelationship of training, supervision, and the quality of
personnel. The data indicated that 64 out of 84 individual items specifically
identified or reinforced the concept of police professionalization. Police
administrators and justice educators definitely viewed police professionalization as being capable of responding to the critical problem of police corruption (More, 1980).

Delphi is a technique that has numerous applications to the justice system
(Delbecq, 1971).

Delbecq

Delbecq is a technique of gathering information from a group of experts.
It uses components of Delphi, but it stresses direct confrontation. The
experts are gathered in a large room and then are divided into small groups.
The facilitator asks everyone to spend thirty minutes defining the topic
(program definition, estimation of future requirements, or whatever) on five
by seven cards. Group members do not discuss their cards.

At the end of thirty minutes, a group recorder is randomly selected and lists one item from each group member card. The recorder writes them on a large pad, without any discussion. The groups are then given a coffee break. Upon returning, each group is given a half hour to discuss their lists. After the thirty minutes, each member of the group is given a three by five card and votes privately on which five items he considers most crucial. The votes are collected and recorded. All groups are gathered together, and a brief discussion follows.

The Delbecq approach was recently compared to a modified nominal group process for public sector problem solving. For an excellent discussion of this, see Etzel (1974).

Roundtable

Roundtable is the traditional approach to expert opinion data gathering. A panel of experts sit around a table and directly discuss or debate the problem, solution, etc. Newman illustrates the roundtable use (Newman, 1972).

For example, the Los Angeles Police Department has implemented the so-called Basic CAR Plan as one way of attaining the department's basic objective of helping society prevent crime through the coordinated efforts of the policeman and the people in the community. The essential idea of the Basic CAR Plan is that the officers assigned to a district meet with the citizens of the district once a month. This enables discussion of police problems between the officers and the citizens and allows for improved understanding of the nature of law enforcement needs and problems as they affect both the officers and the people being served. We asked a group of qualified individuals, specifically members of the 53rd class of the Delinquency Control Institute of the University of Southern California, to serve as experts in this exercise. The Basic CAR Plan was chosen only as an example, and no evaluation was actually intended or carried out. The experts were asked to list what they thought would be the essential criteria for evaluating the effectiveness of this program. Their response is listed under general categories and in order of importance [in Figure IV-3].

Note that there is considerable overlap and that many of these criteria are vague. However, by getting them out before a group they can serve as the starting point for debate.

As a method, roundtable provides a relatively quick technique of achieving a group consensus. However, it also contains certain undesirable psychological factors, such as specious persuasion, the unwillingness to abandon publicly expressed opinions, and the bandwagon effect of majority opinion. Another difficulty is that it cannot be replicated. Notwithstanding its limitations, Julian L. Simon points out that expert opinion will always be an important source of knowledge. (Simon, 1979).

This technique is not limited to before-and-after snapshot measures of a

General	People	Officers
Crime Rate	Attitude of people (youth) toward police	Officers' attitudes/understanding
Reported crime		Reduction in complaints on officers
Is it effective deterrent?	Improved communications between community and police	
Does crime become a neighborhood problem or merely a simple report to police?	Plan accepted by people	Attitude of police toward plan
		Reduction in assaults on officers
What happened to clearance rate?	More or less cooperation by citizenry	Has it raised morale of department?
Number of arrests	Persons reached from criminal element or already cooperative and working with police	Does officer know specific problems on his beat?
Calls for miscellaneous police services	Has it reduced racial tension?	How many citizens known by name by officer on the beat?
Cost versus effectiveness	Attitude change of general public toward its role in law enforcement	Have working conditions for police improved?
		Are more on-sight arrests made?
	Attitude of poor in area	Has it increased efficiency of department?
	Do people relate and identify with officers in assigned area?	
	Hostility towards police	
	Are citizens responding to meetings?	
NOTE: Listed in order of importance and/or popularity	What type of people responding?	

Figure IV-3. Criteria for evaluating a community program.

program. Through the use of the case study, relationships between services and participants may be studied in-depth in order to facilitate insights that may assist the program administrators in improving operations. Case studies are particularly important when inventive, first-of-a-kind programs are tried. Although results from an isolated case study are not generalizable to other programs, they can provide penetrating suggestions for internal program improvements. For a look at the use of case studies in criminal justice application, see *Team Policing—Seven Case Studies,* Police Foundation, Washington, D.C., 1973.

Case studies vary considerably, but their utility is particularly evident (Franklin and Osborne, 1971)

1. where the specific problem is open to research
2. where the problem demands further conceptualization
3. where the problem demands emphasis on the pattern of interpretation given by individuals studied
4. where the problem is to determine the pattern of factors significant to a given case

Case studies are most evident when one reviews the case method utilized by Harvard University (initially created by the Harvard Law School) and developed extensively in the School of Business. The total teaching process utilizes the case method. The cases represent actual situations and are, needless to say, comprehensive and well documented (Pigors, 1967).

In the field of criminal justice, the case study concept has been applied in a few instances, notably by the Inter-University Case Program that developed the following (Inter-University Case Program):

1. Reorganization and Reassignment in the California Highway Patrol, number 75.
2. The Demotion of Deputy Chief Inspector Goldberg, number 78.

The case study optimally represents the essence of objectivity. The case describes the real world (not what should be) and provides the reviewer with the opportunity to learn by independent thought based on critical analysis.

EXPERIMENTAL DATA COLLECTION TECHNIQUES

The last areas to be discussed in this chapter are the myriad of techniques that fall within the framework of the Experimental Method. Some of the most popular ones are documented in this section.

Structured Experiences

The use of structured experiences are primarily aimed at developing learning designs to accomplish stated objectives. The experiences can cover decision making, communication, planning, etc. For example, if one were to address decision making in criminal justice, a structured experience would be developed to assess the impact of individual versus group decision making. In essence, structured experience has a well-defined behavioral goal and is geared toward experimental learning.

Two experts in this area, Michael O'Neill and Kai Martensen, have developed a facilitator's handbook that contains an extensive array of structured experiences. The following is a structured experience that could be utilized by a planner (O'Neill and Martensen, 1975):

Goal Priorities: A Consensus-Seeking Activity

Goals
 I. To assist the group to assess its values.
 II. To focus on the group decision-making process.
 III. To discover evolving leadership in the group.

Group Size

A minimum of three groups and a maximum of five groups, each composed of three to five participants.

Time Required

Approximately one and one-half hours.

Materials

    I. A copy of the summary of the reports of the National Advisory Commission on Criminal Justice Standards and Goals for each participant.

    II. A copy of the Goal Priorities Assessment sheet for each participant.

    III. A copy of the Goal Priorities Observer Form for each observer.

    IV. Newsprint and a felt-tipped marker.

    V. Pencils for all participants.

Physical Setting

A large room with adjacent areas for small groups to meet.

Process

    I. The facilitator distributes to each participant a copy of the standards and goals compiled by the National Advisory Commission on Criminal Justice Standards and Goals. He gives a brief overview of the report.

    II. The facilitator then distributes the Goal Priorities Assessment Sheet and has each participant establish priorities for the goals. (Fifteen minutes)

    III. The participants then form small subgroups to establish priorities for the goals based on group concensus. One member of each subgroup may be the process observer; he receives a copy of the Goal Priorities Observer Form. (Thirty minutes)

Goal Priorities Assessment Sheet

Instructions: Rank the following police goals in order of importance. Place a 1 in front of the most important, a 7 in front of the least important.

Ranking (Priority)

Individual	Group	Goal
_____	_____	To develop fully the potential of the criminal justice system to apprehend offenders.
_____	_____	To establish teamwork between police and citizens.
_____	_____	To establish teamwork among members of the criminal justice system.
_____	_____	To clearly determine and act on the local crime problem.
_____	_____	To make the most of human resources.

_____ _____ To develop full the police response to special community needs.

Goal Priorities Observer Form

1. What value differences were identifiable within the group?
2. How were the differences resolved?
3. Who readily accepted the consensus on priorities? Who did not?
4. How were decisions reached by the group?
5. What *facilitating* leadership behaviors emerged in the discussion?
6. What *inhibiting* leadership behaviors were observed?

Modeling

The use of models help planners describe, predict, or plan. Models have several components that can be discussed as they help depict a state of affairs. The specific techniques that shall be discussed under this broad heading are

1. Models
2. Simulations
3. PERT/CPM network models
4. Queuing Theory

Models

A model can be thought of as a pictorial representation of a problem, program, or system. In this sense, we could describe the model of the Police Adult Intake Decision Points and Alternatives (California Correctional System Intake Study, prepared for the California Department of Corrections) as noted in Figure IV-4. By constructing such a model, we can more effectively assess and understand how a particular system works. The case in point, the police adult intake system. Models provide planners with insights into problems and provide a start for looking at alternatives and their point of impact on the system.

Another model that has been used in some jurisdictions is the Justice System Interactive Model (JUSSIM). The model uses a computer in an *interactive* mode, with a user sitting at a terminal calling a stored data base characterizing the user's criminal justice system and interacting in a conversational way with the computer program, with no special requirements for technical training or computer programming skills, since the entire process goes on in plain English.

The operation of the JUSSIM model can best be explained by examination of a single stage in the flow diagram of cases through a criminal justice

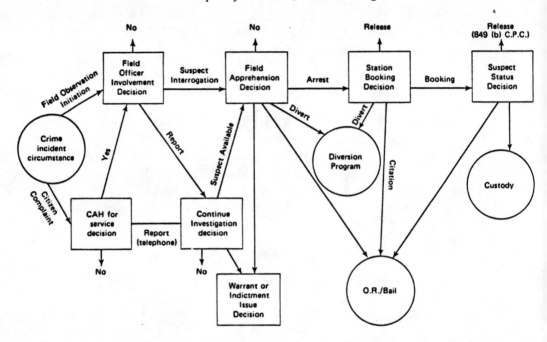

Figure IV-4. Police adult intake points and alternatives.

system. Consider, for example, the jury trial stage for a single crime type (say, robbery). Let us assume for the moment that 100 robbery cases come to the jury trial state, a calculation based on flows from the earlier stages.

As shown in Figure IV-5, there are two output flow paths from the jury trial: *acquittal* and *guilty.* If the branching ratios from jury trial to these two paths are 0.4 (probability of acquittal) and 0.6 (probability of conviction), respectively, then the jury trial stage feeds 60 offenders to the sentencing stage (which also receives offenders coming from guilty plea and bench trial). This same branching and collection process at the earlier stages provided the basis for calculating the 100 cases coming to jury trial. In this simple computation, the branching ratios (the probabilities of conviction and acquittal) are required input data. All input data are shown in Figure IV-5.

We are now interested in calculating the work loads, costs, and resource requirements associated with the two principal resources used to process cases at jury trial: judges and prosecutors. Let us assume that the average *unit workload* for judges in robbery jury trials is six hours, and that the prosecutor (with more preparation time) must spend an average of twenty hours per case.

Focusing on the *judges* now, their *work load* in handling robbery jury trials, at 6 hours per case, for 100 cases is 600 judge-hours. If a judge-hour (including his support staff and facilities) costs $100 (also an input datum),

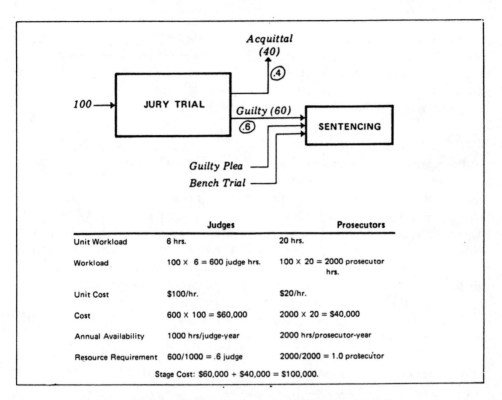

Figure IV-5. An illustrative Jussim stage: Robbery jury trials.

then the cost of the 600 judge-hours is simply $60,000. If a judge is available 1,000 hours per year for processing cases, then the *resource requirement* is the workload (600 judge-hours) divided by this *annual availability*, or 0.6 of a full-time judge is required to process robbery jury trials. Similar computations are made for *prosecutors*, and these are also shown in Figure IV-4.

The robbery jury trial cost, then, is the sum of the resource costs associated with that stage, $60,000 for judges and $40,000 for prosecutors, for a total of $100,000. Similarly, the *court costs* associated with *robbery* can be computed as the sum of the resource costs for all stages in the court system. Then, the *total court costs* would simply be the sum of those costs for all the various types of crime. (Blumstein, 1975).

Simulations

Simulation can best be thought of as a technique of setting up a model or representation of a real situation and then performing variations on it. Role playing of a civil disorder is a form of simulation whereby, under a laboratory situation, alternatives to crowd control or other crime control incidents can be tested. For example, one use of simulation using a computer might evolve around the burglary reduction process. By depicting a model we could simulate alternative measures and try to gauge their impact. It might look like Figure IV-6 (Unwin, 1975). It would be possible by computer simulation to determine what happens if we institute a long-range program. In this way, it would be possible to study the effects of changes in strategies or policies on the burglary reduction process.

PERT

Program evaluation and review technique (PERT) is an extension of the Gantt chart concept. Developed in 1958 by the Navy's Special Project Office and the Lockheed Aircraft Corporation for missile projects, PERT allows the planner greater flexibility than was the case with the Gantt chart. Essentially, it is an analytical device that shows the work necessary to achieve a stated objective/goal while at the same time allowing the planner to predict time and costs under a variety of conditions. It also spotlights those uncertainties or problems that might impede, delay, or frustrate the achievement of the objective/goal.

The focus of PERT is on events or activities. The event is the specific achievement or accomplishment. The activity is the work that is necessary to achieve or accomplish the event(s). The events and activities are laid out in a network. For a hypothetical Sheriff's Department communication network, a PERT network would look like Figure IV-7.

The very first step involved in PERT is developing the network. The planner simply estimates all the events and activities that are necessary to achieve a certain goal. In the hypothetical sheriff's department communication center, the steps could be the following:

1. Building—design and construct on county property
2. Equipment—design, set specifications, accept bids, choose, order, receive, and install equipment in new building
3. Personnel—(1) train presently employed in new equipment; (2) train personnel transferred from other agencies in S.O. policies, etc., and in new equipment; and (3) recruit, select, and train the additional personnel to be hired

The planner can make the PERT network as simple or as complex as he desires. Often the general plan is kept simple, and the appendices to the plan contain the more complex steps.

After the network's steps (events and activities) are laid out, the planner now calculates which events/activities can occur concurrently and which must await the completion of other steps. For instance, the hypothetical communication center cannot be tested until building, equipment, and personnel are ready. The acquisition of equipment can, however, occur

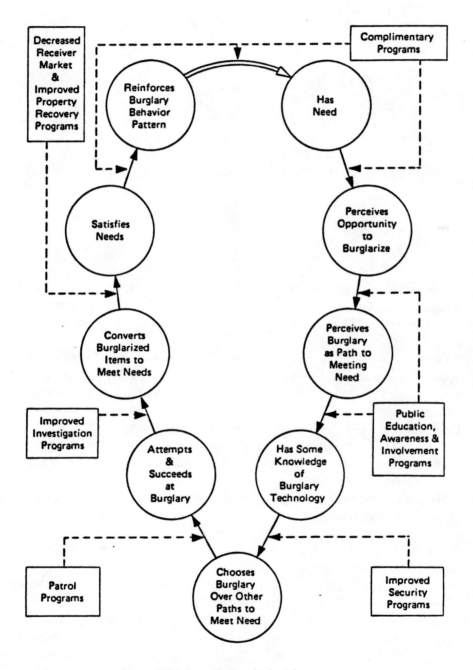

Figure IV-6. Interdicting the burglary system.

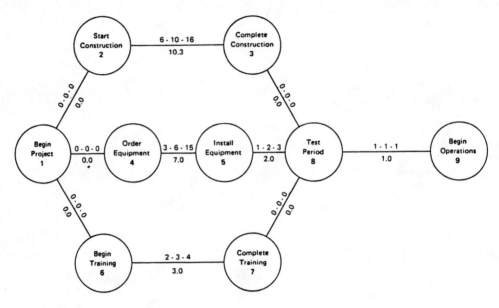

Figure IV-7. PERT network.

concurrently with either the training of personnel or the construction of the building. The desire is to have the building completed and personnel trained at the same time. That way neither the personnel nor the building are sitting idle.

Once the logical flow of events are laid out, the planner begins to collect information on *time*. The responsibilities (i.e., contractor, equipment suppliers, trainers, etc.) are contacted and three *times* are solicited. These are their estimated *optimistic time* (t_o), *most likely time* (t_m), and *pessimistic time* (t_p). These *times* are then written onto the network in the t_o-t_m-t_p order. So if our hypothetical contractor estimates six weeks as his optimistic, ten weeks for his most likely, and sixteen weeks for his pessimistic, these times are placed on the network.

Since the times solicited are in weeks, the same unit is used throughout. The reader has probably noticed some activities have estimated times of *0–0–0* and *1–1–1*. The *0–0–0* is simply a dummy activity inserted in the network to maintain the logical sequence of events. In activity 7–8, there is no time needed from those completing training to the beginning of the test of man, machine, and building. The *1–1–1* of activity 8–9 simply is the estimator allowing one week for tests—no more and no less.

Once these time estimates are completed, the planner needs to know exactly the amount of time each activity is expected to take. The expected time (t_e) is calculated from the t_o-t_m-t_p by using the following formula:

$$\frac{t_o + 4t_m + t_p}{6}$$

This formula is derived from empirical investigation and is the weighted average of all three times. There is a 50–50 chance that more or less time will be required. So, the estimated time (t_e) for the times given by the contractor on the building would be (activity 2–3) 10.3 weeks.

With the optimistic/most likely/pessimistic $(t_o$-t_m-$t_p)$ times as well as the expected time (t_e) available, the planner can easily calculate and give an inquirer an estimate of how long the plan or project will take, from start to finish. By adding up the times in our hypothetical case and using the largest figure, the planner will be *in the ball park*.

Several other calculations can be made by the planner using the PERT network. If one wants to know when an event can be expected to be completed, or the earliest expected time (t_e), the planner simply adds up the expected times (t_e) for event 8 on path 1–4–5–8, which is 9.0 weeks. For path 1–6–7–8, it is 3.0 weeks. The planner knows he can begin the activities of path 1–6–7–8 $(t_e = 3.0)$ three weeks prior to the completion of path 1–4–5–8 $(t_e = 9.0)$; to begin path 1–6–7–8 earlier would mean the people trained to communicate would *sit around* until the building is completed—a wasted resource. The planner may also want to know the times when each event should begin in order to meet any *target* date for the project's completion. Called the latest allowable time (Tl), the expected times (t_e) for each activity is subtracted back from the target date. So, if we want our hypothetical communications facility operational on July 1st, then event 5 must begin three weeks prior to that date (path 5–8–9, t_e 2 + 1 = 3).

Critical Path Method .

The Critical Path Method (CPM) is the path with the longest times. It is determined by simply adding up all the expected times (t_e) of each path. The planner uses the t_e (expected time), since it is the weighted average. If the pessimistic time (t_p) was used, then path 1–4–5–8–9 would be critical, but PERT planners have found the use of expected time (t_e) better. Mathematicians say the odds are 100 to 1 that optimistic (t_o) or pessimistic (t_p) times will actually occur. In our hypothetical case, the critical path would then be 1–2–3–8–9, which has a total t_e of 11.3 weeks.

For the criminal justice system planner who must accelerate the program to meet a newer and shorter deadline than originally anticipated, this would mean concentrating resources on shortening the time involved in path 1–2–3–8–9. Placing calculable resources elsewhere while giving the idea of speeding up the project would not accomplish the purpose. The fact that activities have been speeded up on the wrong path has probably contributed to the saying *hurry up and wait.* By PERT-ing out the activities, the critical path can be discovered and the *pressure* brought to bear on the right places, if haste is required.

Queuing Theory

Queuing is a mathematical technique which deals with problems of congestion. Queuing problems arise when service demands exceed the rate at which a required service can be provided. The applicability of queuing to the patrol force of a police department or servicing customers in a records section would present typical queuing problems. For an in-depth look into queuing application in police work, see *Urban Police Patrol Analysis,* by Larsons, R. C., MIT Press, 1972.

In this chapter, emphasis has been placed on a discussion of numerous techniques applicable to the three methods of data collection. In the next chapter, consideration is given to a detailed analysis of the planning process.

TOPICS FOR DISCUSSION

1. Describe the techniques applicable to baseline data collection, field data collection and experimental data collection.
2. Select a problem and demonstrate the use of PERT.
3. List and discuss applications in criminal justice planning that might be enhanced by the use of the Delphi Technique.
4. Discuss how Delphi differs from Delbecq.
5. List and describe several of the most commonly used statistics.
6. Describe a typical model as it is applied to criminal justice.
7. Identify the characteristics of a structured experience.

REFERENCES

Anderson, Theodore and Zeldatch, Morris. *A Basic Course in Statistics: With Sociological Implications,* 2nd ed. New York: Holt, Rinehart and Winston, Inc., 1968.

Blumstein, Alfred. A model to aid in planning for the total criminal justice system. In Oberlander, Leonard, Editor, *Quantitative Tools for Criminal Justice Planning.* Washington, D.C.: G.P.O., 1975.

Dalker, Norman C. *Delphi.* Santa Monica, California: The Rand Corporation, 1968.

Delbecq, Andrew and Vande Ven, Andrew. A group process model for problem identification and program planning. *Journal of Applied Behavioral Sciences,* 7:466, 1971.

Edwards, Allen. *Statistical Methods,* 2nd ed. New York: Holt, Rinehart and Winston, Inc., 1967.

Etzel, Michael, et al. A modified nominal-group process for public sector problem solving. *Public Personnel Management Journal,* 6:439, 1974.

Forst, Brian. Statistical techniques and their limitations in the analysis of criminal justice data.

In Oberlander, Leonard, Editor. *Quantitative Tools for Criminal Justice Planning.* Washington, D.C.: G.P.O., 1975.

Franklin, Billy J., and Osborne, Harold W., Editors. *Research Methods: Issues and Insights.* Belmont, California: Wadsworth Publishing Co., 1971.

Gordon, T. J. and Helmer, Olaf. *Report on a Long Range Forecasting Study.* Santa Monica, California: Rand Corporation, 1964.

Illinois Law Enforcement Commission. *Evaluation of the Illinois Crime Laboratory System.* Unpublished report, January, 1975.

Issac, Stephen. *Handbook in Research and Evaluation.* San Diego, California: Robert O. Knapp, Publisher, 1974.

Kraemer, Kenneth. *Policy Analysis in Local Government.* Washington, D.C.: International City Management Association, 1973.

Krippendorff, Klaus. *Content Analysis,* Beverly Hills: Sage Publications, 1980.

Larsons, R. C. *Urban Police Patrol Analysis.* Boston: MIT Press, 1972.

More, Harry W., Jr. Delphi analysis of police corruption. *Journal of Police Science and Administration,* 8:107, 1980.

Morrow, James. *A Delphi Approach to the Future of Management.* Ann Arbor, MI: University Microfilms, 1972.

National Advisory Commission on Criminal Justice Standards and Goals. *Criminal Justice System.* Washington, D.C.: U.S. Government Printing Office, 1973.

National Institute of Law Enforcement and Criminal Justice. *Publications of the National Institute of Law Enforcement and Criminal Justice.* Washington, D.C.: G.P.O., 1978.

Newman, Robert, and Jollee, Aberstone. *Evaluation Technology.* A report prepared for the Los Angeles Regional Criminal Justice Planning Board, January, 1972.

O'Neill, Michael, and Martensen, Kai. *Criminal Justice Group Training — A Facilitated Handbook.* La Jolla, California: University Associates, 1975.

Selltiz, Claire, Jahoda, Marie, Deutsch, Morton, and Cook, Stuart W. *Research Methods in Social Relations.* New York: Holt, Rinehart and Winston, 1959.

Simon, Julian L. *Basic Research Methods in Social Science.* New York: Random House, 1969.

Team Policing — Seven Case Studies. Washington, D.C.: Police Foundation, 1973.

Unsinger, Peter. Discussion paper of PERT prepared for San Jose State University Police Middle Management Programs, unpublished, 1974.

Unwin, Ernest (Consultant). *A Seminar Training Paper.* unpublished, 1975.

Chapter V

COLLECTION AND ANALYSIS OF DATA

The previous chapters have discussed the basic frame of reference for criminal justice planning. In this chapter, emphasis is placed on several data collection methods available to the criminal justice planner and the type of analysis that the planner can perform.

The framework for the collection and analysis of data is based on three collection classifications:

1. Baseline
2. Field
3. Experimental

DATA COLLECTION METHODS

The methods of data collection for the criminal justice system can be categorized into three classifications; baseline, field, and experimental. Each of these methods has a subset methodology to both collect and analyze the data. This discussion will focus on the methods and subsets only, since the techniques are discussed at length in Chapter IV.

The method of data collection refers to the place that data is usually collected. For example, baseline data involves library research. Field data collection consists of collecting data in the field by survey or other research techniques. Experimental data collection refers to *laboratory* type collection efforts. An example might be to collect data on the use of stress training for police officers, with a control and experimental group of officers. Figure V-1 indicates the three classifications as they relate to these or procedures that are used to collect the data. As can be seen by the figure, these include observations, questionnaires, interviews, etc.

In the field of criminal justice there is a mystique and unawareness about the types of data obtainable.

PRIMARY BASELINE DATA SOURCES

There are two primary sources of nationwide statistical data on the nature and extent of criminal activity in the United States. The *Uniform Crime*

Method	Sub Set Method (Procedures)	(Techniques)
Baseline Data Collection	Analysis of historical records, criminal justice management reports, UCR reports.	Taking notes. Descriptive or content analysis.
	Analysis of agency documents, statistical and non-statistical agency records.	Statistical compilation and manipulation.
		Graphs.
		Charts.
	Literature search for previous research or theories that would impact on the criminal justice problem defined. Research books, journals, National Criminal Justice Reference Service.	
Field Data Collection	Questionnaire	Use of attitudinal scales to measure agency performance
	Interview	job satisfaction, morale.
	Case Study	Content analysis.
	Observation	Use of opinions recording behavior.
	Expert Opinion	Delphi or other appropriate method.
Experimental	Small group study, problem solving, control groups. Program experimentation.	Use of structural experiences; pilot tests. Use of observers. Use of simulation, modeling, senarios, etc.

Figure V-1. Classification of data. Adopted from: Mike Woodcock and Dave Francis, eds. *Unblocking Your Organization*. San Diego, Ca: University Associates, Inc., 1979. Used with permission.

Reports, issued annually by the Federal Bureau of Investigation, reports the volume and rate of crimes known to the police. These data are compiled by the FBI on the basis of information provided by local law enforcement agencies throughout the United States. Another source of data on the nature and extent of crime is the annual series of reports of the *National Crime Survey,* conducted by the United States Bureau of the Census for the Bureau of Justice Statistics. The *National Crime Survey* data, derived from interviews with samples of households designed to be representative of the Nation, report on the estimated number and rate of personal and household victimizations.

These data are supplemented by a variety of data derived from self-report surveys on drug and alcohol use, gambling, and other illegal activities that are reported by several organizations. Agencies with specialized law enforcement functions, such as the Securities and Exchange Commission, Postal Inspection Service, Drug Enforcement Administration, Secret Service, and others collect statistical information on case processing and agency activities. In addition, private organizations such as the Association of American Railroads, American Humane Association, and National Education Association publish data on various forms of illegal activity related to their organizational purposes.

Information on personnel and expenditures for the criminal justice system is found in a variety of sources. Government publications, such as the *Budget of the United States Government* and agency annual reports, provide data on expenditures for criminal justice-related activities. The Bureau of Justice Statistics' publication, *Expenditure and Employment Data for the Criminal Justice System,* compiles data on criminal justice agency personnel, payroll, and expenditure. Various special surveys, such as the *Census of Local Jails,* the *Census of State Correctional Facilities,* and the *State Salary Survey* of probation and parole personnel conducted by the U.S. Office of Personnel Management contain information on personnel, source of funding, and expenditures for these segments of the criminal justice system. These sources are augmented by surveys conducted by the National Center for State Courts, the National Council on Crime and Delinquency, the American Correctional Association, the Fraternal Order of Police, and other groups.

Data on clearance and arrest rates are provided primarily by the *Uniform Crime Reports.* In addition, agencies such as the Drug Enforcement Administration, Immigration and Naturalization Service, and others collect data on clearances and arrests in cases under their jurisdiction.

Court-related data for the federal system come from the Administrative Office of the U.S. Courts and the Federal Prison System. Although no uniform standardized court reporting system (comparable to the *Uniform Crime Reports*) currently exists at the State level, in the past the National Center for State Courts' publication, *State Court Caseload Statistics,* contained state-by-state information relating to the activities of state courts.

Data on probation systems are provided by the American Correctional Association. Information on correctional institutions is found in a number of sources, including the *Prisoners in State and Federal Institutions* series published by the Bureau of Justice Statistics, as well as in special purpose reports such as the *Survey of Inmates of State Correctional Facilities.* Information on Federal prisoners is available in the annual *Statistical Report* of the Federal Prison System. In addition to these sources, data on prison populations and characteristics of correctional facilities and inmates are provided by surveys conducted by the American Correctional Association and numerous private research groups and individual researchers.

Statistics on parole services are collected and reported by the *Uniform Parole Reports* program of the National Council on Crime and Delinquency, the American Correctional Association, and the U.S. Parole Commission. Discharges from state and federal correctional facilities are reported in the *Prisoners in State and Federal Institutions* series issued by the Bureau of Justice Statistics.

In the juvenile justice system, data on offenses and on juveniles taken into custody are reported by the Federal Bureau of Investigation's *Uniform Crime Reports*. Data on the volume of cases disposed of by juvenile courts are provided in *Delinquency 1978*, by the National Center for Juvenile Justice.

Juvenile correctional data are provided by a number of sources. The *Children in Custody* series issued by the Office of Juvenile Justice and Delinquency Prevention reports data on the number of juveniles held in public and private juvenile correctional facilities. In addition, the American Correctional Association collects data on juvenile correctional facilities, probation and parole officers, and juveniles under correctional supervision. There is no nationwide reporting system that collects data on parole (*aftercare*) outcome for juveniles. (Sourcebook of Criminal Justice Statistics, 1982.)

SOURCEBOOK OF CRIMINAL JUSTICE STATISTICS

One notable source that has compiled criminal justice data from a myriad of compilations is the *Source Book of Criminal Justice Statistics* (see Figure V-2).

The data included in the *Sourcebook* is divided into six sections. The first, *Characteristics of the Criminal Justice Systems*, includes data on the number and types of criminal justice agencies and employees, criminal justice expenditures, workload of agency personnel, and so on. This section also includes most of the tables that summarize statutory, regulatory, or administrative characteristics or practices of criminal justice agencies on a state-by-state basis. The next section, *Public Attitudes Toward Crime and Criminal Justice-Related Topics*, contains the results of nationwide public opinion polls on subjects such as fear of victimization, the death penalty, wiretaps, gun control, drug use, and evaluation of law enforcement, judicial, and correctional agency performance. In the third section, *Nature and Distribution of Known Offenses*, data on several indicators of the extent of illegal activities can be found. These include proportions of persons reporting that they have used various drugs, surveys of individuals, households, and businesses that may have been victims of crimes, and law enforcement agency counts of offenses reported to them. The fourth section, *Characteristics and Distribution of Persons Arrested*, includes counts of arrestees by age, sex, race, and area, proportions of known crimes cleared by arrests, and counts of illegal goods seized. *Judicial Processing of*

CRIME AND LAW

(1) Criminal and civil justice agencies
(1) Expenditures, employment and payroll for criminal justice programs
(1) Expenditures, federal employment and payroll for criminal justice activities
(1) Characteristics of crime victim compensation programs
(1) Characteristics of child sexual abuse legislation
(1) Characteristics of intermittent confinement
(1) Characteristics of privacy legislation
(1) Characteristics of gun control legislation
(1) Characteristics of marihuana legislation
(2) Attitudes toward extent of crime
(2) Attitudes toward safety in the home
(2) Attitudes toward safety on the streets
(2) Fear of crime
(2) Crime prevention precautions employed
(2) Attitudes toward selected social issues
(2) Attitudes toward causes of crime
(2) Attitudes toward methods of dealing with crime
(2) Attitudes toward legalization of abortion
(2) Attitudes toward confidentiality of news sources
(2) Gun ownership
(2) Attitudes toward gun control
(2) Attitudes toward the use and effect of drugs and alcohol
(2) Attitudes toward legalization of marihuana
(2) Attitudes toward forbidding the sale of alcohol
(2) Attitudes toward pornography
(3) Estimated number of personal household and business victimizations
(3) Estimated percentage of non-reported personal and household victimizations
(3) Estimated rate of personal and household victimizations
(3) Estimated number of personal and household incidents by specific incident characteristics
(3) Estimated number of personal victimizations by specific incident characteristics
(3) Estimated rate and number of household victimizations
(3) Changes in rates of personal and household victimizations between 1973 and 1980
(3) Households touched by crime between 1975 and 1981
(3) Child abuse characteristics of reports victims and perpetrators
(3) Estimated number of personal victimizations of teachers
(3) Reported alcohol use
(3) Reported drug use among adults and youth
(3) Offenses known to the police
(3) Offenses in U.S. park areas
(3) Murders known to the police
(3) Robberies known to the police
(3) Aggravated assaults known to the police
(3) Burglaries known to the police
(3) Larcenies known to the police
(3) Violations of federal bank robbery statutes
(3) Motor vehicle thefts known to the police
(3) Property loss due to selected crimes
(3) Federal officers killed and assaulted
(3) Law enforcement officers killed
(3) Persons identified as killing law enforcement officers
(3) Assaults on law enforcement officers
(3) Drug thefts and illegal drug prices
(3) Bombing incidents known to the police
(3) International terrorist incidents against U.S. citizens and property
(3) Hijackings and other criminal acts related to air transportation
(3) Crime insurance policies, claims, and losses
(3) Offenses against railroads

POLICE

(1) Employment and payroll for police services
(1) Salaries and employment characteristics of State police
(1) Characteristics of crime victim compensation
(1) Attitudes toward performance of police
(2) Attitudes toward police use of force
(2) Attitudes toward deterrent effect of the law enforcement system
(4) Arrests, national estimates
(4) Number and rate of arrests
(4) Characteristics of persons arrested
(4) Arrests in cities
(4) Arrests in suburban areas
(4) Arrests in rural areas
(4) Arrest rates
(4) Clearance rates
(4) Arrests for alcohol-related offenses
(4) Arrests, self-report data
(4) Juvenile offenders taken into police custody
(4) Arrests for drug law violations
(4) Drug Seizures
(4) Seizures by the U.S. Customs Service
(4) Aliens deported from the United States
(4) Activities of the U.S. Secret Service
(4) Arrests for offenses against railroads
(4) Criminal investigations by the U.S. Postal Inspection Service

PROSECUTION AND DEFENSE

(1) Expenditures, workload, employment, and payroll for defense activities
(1) Employment and payroll for legal services and prosecution activities
(1) Employment and salaries of attorney generals' offices
(5) Requests for immunity by federal prosecutors
(5) Cases argued and pending in U.S. Attorney's offices
(5) Antitrust cases filed in U.S. District Courts
(5) Cases referred to the U.S. Department of Justice for prosecution by the Securities and Exchange Commission
(5) Prosecutions of violations of immigration and nationality laws
(5) Prosecutions of corrupt officials

COURTS

(1) Expenditures, employment, payroll, and salaries of federal judicial and court administrative personnel
(1) Workload and duties of the federal judiciary
(1) Characteristics of presidential appointees to federal judgeships
(1) Expenditures, employment, and payroll for State judicial activities
(1) Qualification requirements, salaries, selection process, and terms of office of trial and appellate judges
(1) Expenditures for and utilization of grand and petit jurors
(1) Statutory provisions governing age for juvenile court jurisdiction
(1) Statutory provisions governing waiver of juveniles to criminal court
(2) Public confidence in the U.S. Supreme Court
(2) Attitudes toward severity of courts
(5) Delinquency cases disposed of by juvenile courts
(5) Court authorized interception of wire or oral communication
(5) Cases filed in U.S. District Courts
(5) Proposed and actual time limits for judicial processing
(5) Defendants disposed of in U.S. District Courts
(5) Prisoner petitions filed in U.S. District Courts
(5) Appeals filed in U.S. Courts of Appeals
(5) Petitions for writ of certiorari to the U.S. Supreme Court
(5) Executive clemency applications
(5) Dispositions and sentences of defendants charged with drug law violations in U.S. District Courts
(5) Dispositions of persons arrested for offenses against railroads
(5) Dispositions in criminal tax fraud cases
(5) Dispositions of arrests by the U.S. Secret Service
(5) Military
  Army personnel tried and convicted in U.S. Army General and Special Courts-Martial
  Air Force personnel tried and convicted on U.S. Air Force General and Special Courts-Martial
  Navy and Marine Corps personnel tried and convicted in U.S. Navy and Marine Corps General and Special Courts-Martial
  Coast Guard personnel tried in U.S. Coast Guard Special Courts-Martial

CORRECTIONS

(1) Expenditures, employment, and payroll for correctional activities
(1) Employment, workload, and salaries for probation/parole officers
(1) Characteristics of public and private juvenile facilities, staff, and residents
(1) Utilization of drug abuse treatment programs
(1) Employment of and salaries for State correctional units
(1) Unionization of State correctional officers
(1) Characteristics of adult correctional and pre-release facilities
(1) Mental health staff and services in adult correctional facilities
(1) Workload of U.S. Parole Commission hearing examiners
(1) Representation at parole consideration and revocation hearings
(1) Statutory regulations on deinstitutionalization of juveniles
(2) Attitudes toward deterrent effect of prison sentences
(2) Attitudes toward purposes of imprisonment
(2) Attitudes toward capital punishment
(6) Persons under supervision of the Federal Probation System
(6) Drug users admitted to federally-funded drug abuse treatment programs
(6) Characteristics of public and private juvenile custody facilities
(6) Number and rate of inmates in local jails and characteristics of jail inmates
(6) Number and rate of sentenced prisoners under 18 years of age in adult correctional facilities
(6) Prisoners in, rates of incarceration for, admissions to, and movement of prisoners in State and federal institutions
(6) Characteristics of inmates in State correctional facilities
(6) Use of Pell Grants by inmates in State institutions
(6) Movement of prisoners in, admissions to and releases from federal correctional facilities
(6) Population of U.S. Army, U.S. Navy, and U.S. Marine Corps correctional facilities
(6) Residents in pre-release facilities
(6) Releases from State and federal institutions
(6) Movement of prisoners paroled and conditionally released from State and federal institutions
(6) Deaths among prisoners under the jurisdiction of State and federal correctional authorities
(6) Capital punishment
  Prisoners under sentence of death
  State and federal prisoners executed

Figure V-2. Sourcebook of criminal justice statistics.

Defendants, the fifth section, contains information on the number of juveniles and adults processed through the courts, as well as the characteristics, dispositions, and sentences of the defendants. Finally, the sixth section, *Persons Under Correctional Supervision,* provides data about persons on probation and parole, population and movement of inmates of federal institutions, and characteristics of state prison inmates. This section also presents data on offenders executed, as well as offenders currently under sentence of death. Each of these six major sections (into which the Sourcebook is divided) is introduced by brief comments giving a more detailed overview of the data contained in that section (*Sourcebook of Criminal Justice Statistics,* 1982).

It can readily be seen that statistical information about crime and the criminal justice system in the United States is gathered and published by hundreds of operating agencies, academic institutions, research organizations, public opinion polling firms, and other groups. These sources of data represent both the private and public sector, and within the public sector, the many levels of government that are involved in the collection and dissemination of criminal justice statistical data.

A primary source of data that should not be overlooked is that of professional journals. A comprehensive list of criminal justice journals will vary (based on the perspective of the classifier), but should clearly represent the total system rather than an undue emphasis on one segment. Figure V-3 lists a number of journals that provide a broad coverage of the justice environment.

Criminology

Crime and Delinquency

Journal of Criminal Justice

Journal of Police Science and Administration

Criminal Law Bulletin

Victimology

Federal Probation

Judicature

American Journal of Corrections

Justice Systems Journal

Police Chief

California Law Enforcement Journal

Crime Prevention Review

Police Studies

FBI Law Enforcement Bulletin

Criminal Justice and Behavior

Figure V-3. Criminal justice journals.

The National Institute of Justice published numerous documents that are of considerable interest to criminal justice planners. Typical of these is the *Police Research Catalog* that annotates research supported by the government from 1969 to 1981 (National Institute of Justice, 1982). A subject index of this publication is set forth in Figure V-4. While this reference is limited to a review of police topics, other documents can be obtained that address other segments of the justice system.

Automated Police Information Systems	Police Manpower Deployment
Automated Vehicle Monitors	Police Occupational Stress
Blood and Body Fluid Analysis	Police Patrol
Crime Laboratories	Police Prosecutor Relations
Criminal Investigation	Police Resource Allocation
Criminalistics	Police Response Time
Drug Law Enforcement	Police Role
Evidence Identification and Analysis	Police Telecommunications Systems
Hair and Fiber Analysis	Police Training
Interagency Cooperation	Police Unions
Personnel Administration	Police Use of Deadly Force
Planning	Police Weapons
Police Cars	Polygraph
Police Community Relations	Private Security
Police Corruption	Public Attitudes
Police Crisis Intervention	Rural Crime
Police Effectiveness	Specialized Police Operations
Police Equipment/Technology	Traffic Accidents
Police Management	Work Attitudes

Figure V-4. Police related research (1969–1981).

The sources of data that can be used by criminal justice planners are varied, but one that is unique and should be included in every planner's databank is the *Selective Notification of Information* (see Figure V-5). This is a program of the United States Department of Justice and announces the most significant documents and audiovisual materials added to the data base of the National Institute of Justice/NCJRS during the previous two months. NCJRS—the National Criminal Justice Reference Service—is a national and international clearinghouse of law enforcement and criminal justice information. NCJRS adds more than 1,000 items to its automated data base bimonthly. SNI provides bibliographic descriptions, abstracts, and availability information for approximately 5 percent of these acquisitions. SNI helps keep you at the state of the art by announcing reports of research and other current literature.

This agency distributes microfiche copies of many documents without charge. All documents distributed by NCJRS are also reproduced on microfiche. When documents distributed by other sources are also available on

ALTERNATIVES TO INSTITUTIONALIZATION
Organization and Operations
Community-Based Corrections (Adult), Community-Based Corrections (Juvenile), Rehabilitation and Treatment (Community Based)

COURTS
Organization and Administration
Bail and Bond, Court Management and Operations, Court Structure, Judicial process, Support Services (Provided by Courts)

CRIME DETERRENCE
Operations
Crime Deterrence and Prevention (Deterrence), Environmental Design (Effects of), Security Systems (Effects of)

CRIME PREVENTION
Operations
Community Involvement (for Crime Prevention), Crime Deterrence and Prevention (Prevention)

CRIMINALISTICS AND FORENSICS
Organization and Operations
Criminalistics, Forensics

CRIMINOLOGY
Theories and Research
Behavioral and Social Sciences, Crime Causes, Criminology, Research and Development, Victimization

DEFENSE
Organization and Operations
Defense Services, Support Services (Defense)

DRUG ABUSE
Theories and Methods
Alcoholism, Drug Information, Drug Treatment

EVALUATION
Issues and Methods
Planning and Evaluation (Evaluation)

FACILITY DESIGN
Application and Evaluation
Environmental Design (Technology)

FRAUD/WASTE/ABUSE OF PUBLIC FUNDS
Prevention and Detection
Audit, Detection, Investigation, Prevention, Internal and Management Control Systems, Inspector General, Legislative Audit, Other Control Units, Offenses, including Corruption, White-Collar Crime, Fraud on the Government, and Computer-Related Crime and Abuse

INSTITUTIONAL CORRECTIONS (ADULT)
Organization and Operations
Classification of Offenders, Correctional Institutions (Adult), Correctional Management (Adult), Jails, Prison Disorders, Rehabilitation and Treatment (Adult Institutions)

INSTITUTIONAL CORRECTIONS (JUVENILE)
Organization and Operations
Correctional Institutions (Juvenile), Correctional Management (Juvenile), Rehabilitation and Treatment (Juvenile Institutions)

JUVENILE JUSTICE SYSTEM
Systems and Operations
Juvenile Court, Juvenile Delinquency

OFFENSES
Descriptions of Criminal Activity
Classification of Crime, Gambling, Organized Crime, Riot Control and Urban Disorders, Student Disorders, Terrorism, Victimless Crimes, White-Collar Crime, Domestic Violence

POLICE
Organization and Operations
Criminal Investigation, Police Internal Affairs, Police Management, Police Organization, Police Patrol Function, Police Resource Allocation, Police Traffic Function

POLICY AND PLANNING
Issues and Policies
Costs of Crime, Financial Management, Laws and Statutes, Planning and Evaluation (Planning), Privacy and Security

PROBATION AND PAROLE
Organization and Operations
Pardon, Probation and Parole (Adult), Probation and Parole (Juvenile), Rehabilitation and Treatment (Probation and Parole)

PROSECUTION
Organization and Operations
Prosecution, Support Services (Prosecution)

PUBLIC INVOLVEMENT
Techniques and Programs
Community Involvement, Community Relations, Public Information and Education

REFERENCE AND STATISTICS
Reference Material, Statistics

STAFF RESOURCE DEVELOPMENT
Theory and Programs
Civil Rights, Education (Career), Indian Affairs, Training, Personnel Administration

TECHNOLOGY
Application and Evaluation
Communications (Equipment Data, Visual, Voice), Explosives and Weapons, Information Systems Software, Police Equipment, Security Systems (Technology)

Figure V-5. Subject areas included in the selective notification of information.

microfiche from NCJRS, this information is included in the availability statement after the abstract. To order microfiche from NCJRS, specify the title and NCJ number of the document, include a self-addressed mailing label, and mail to:

> National Institute of Justice/NCJRS
> Microfiche Program
> Box 6000, Rockville, MD 20850

In addition, all publications announced in SNI and all documents in the NCJRS collection may be borrowed for four weeks from NCJRS through interlibrary loan. Documents are not loaned directly to individuals. To take advantage of the National Institute of Justice/NCJRS Document Loan Program, request a loan through your public, organizational, or academic library. Give your library the complete title and NCJ number, and ask the librarian to submit the standard interlibrary loan form to:

> National Institute of Justice/NCJRS
> Document Loan Program
> Box 6000, Rockville, MD 20850

In a recent review of sources of basic criminal justice statistics, Eugene Doleschal, Director of the National Council on Crime and Delinquency Information Center, reported that the availability of statistical data on crime and criminal justice in the United States ranges from a total lack of fundamental figures on some subjects to extensive, exotic minutia on others. Moreover, the review reported that the coverage of these data is neither uniform, regular, nor comparable in terms of reporting over time and across political subdivisions (Sources of Basic Criminal Justice Statistics, 1979).

The need for basic criminal justice statistics is becoming more apparent, but other areas are similarly deficient. There is a continuing and urgent need for internal management information. As the cost of operating the criminal justice system increases and tax revenues become more scarce, agencies are under increasing pressure to operate at maximum efficiency. Cutback management is becoming the byword of the day in many agencies. Managers, therefore, require data that enable them to measure performance and to make maximum use of available resources.

Heads of criminal justice agencies need a variety of data to support budget preparation and control, personnel administration, and resource management. Police agencies are concerned with the functional distribution of personnel into specialized units such as patrol, investigative, traffic, juvenile, and administration (Leonard and More, 1982). Courts are confronted with decision making in the allocation of resources, calendering, and jury utilization. In the field of corrections, data dealing with the projected needs of jails and prisons must be collected and evaluated.

Reliable information for decision making gives the manager the opportunity to perform with increasing effectiveness in a changing environment. Justice management is moving rapidly from a *fly-by-the-seat-of-the-pants* reaction to crises to a position in which the executive is making decisions based on scientifically derived knowledge (Robinson, 1969).

ANALYSIS OF DATA

After data have been collected, they must be compiled and rearranged to make them yield the information they contain. This is the process of data analysis.

Many different processes in criminal justice are called *analysis.* What type of analysis a manager/planner does depends upon the type of question to be answered, the method by which data is collected, and the viability of the question or hypothesis that has been formulated.

A good analysis shows the important data in a clearly understandable form so the meaning is easily grasped by the reader. For example, there should be a separate table or graph for each point you are trying to make, rather than one enormous master compilation in which nothing is obvious.

The more complicated processes of analysis take place in causal and noncausal relationship research and in comparison research. Regardless of the type of problem or the processes used for its solution, work must begin with a careful consideration of the criminal justice problem.

It is difficult to specify a possible answer to a specific problem. It is much easier to wave your hands and in vagueness state: "*I'm interested in getting some answers about juvenile delinquency.*" What answers? To what questions? Do you want to know how many juvenile delinquents there are? Or whether separated parents affect the rate of juvenile delinquency? Or whether or not juvenile delinquents delight in their delinquency? Or what? Each of these questions can still be further defined to aid the planner.

The preceding discussion applies to all data collection efforts. An excellent illustration of this appeared in a federal document that addressed the topics of scientific method and research methodology (National Advisory Commission on Criminal Justice Standards and Goals, 1973). Its findings are discussed in this chapter.

The fundamental system of thinking and action that permeates processes of effective program evaluation is the philosophy of inquiry or the application of the scientific method to guide observations, measurements, and evaluations of data. This philosophy postulates the procedures and techniques of scientific research for gaining knowledge. It also proposes a certain attitude—the empirical attitude—that searches for and relies on objective factual observations and evidence.

In addition to its empirical base, the scientific method is systematic. Conducted according to a comprehensive plan (the research design), it not only specifies what to observe, but looks for relationships, patterns, and order between observations. It also supplies the power of self-correction via built-in controls that help verify the reliability and validity of the data attained. *Control* means the ability to isolate and assess the fluctuation of variables that are relevant to what is being observed.

Research investigations are open, explicit, and reproducible while the assumptions, values, calculations, limitations, and conclusions are documented and susceptible to testing, criticism, and refutation.

Every administrator within the criminal justice system should possess a working knowledge of the philosophy of the scientific method and how this method can be harnessed to enhance the process of program evaluation. Essentially, the scientific method requires the following:

1. Reliance on facts. *Facts* refers to events that may be directly observed and replicated. (*Evidence* could be substituted for facts.)
2. Use of systems analysis in comprehending complex phenomena. Analysis involves division of system or program into the specific procedures and operations for purposes of assessment, design, and redesign.
3. Development of hypotheses to guide research. Hypotheses are careful, explicit predictions of outcomes that can be tested against observations.
4. Depersonalization or freedom from bias, and the subjectivity that characterizes commonsense convictions.
5. Objective measurement. Knowledge expands in large part through the development and refinement of instruments of measurement.
6. Quantitative methods to treat data. The main concepts are operationally defined; that is, the activities performed to manipulate and measure a concept are specified in quantifiable terms. Additionally, the objective language of statistics is channeled to analyze, classify, and summarize data (National Advisory Commission on Criminal Justice Standards and Goals, 1973).

RESEARCH DESIGN

Scientific research is not complex. It is simply a series of specific efforts to obtain reliable knowledge in accordance with specific guidelines or steps (Robinson, 1969).

A research design constitutes a blueprint for the collection, measurement, and analysis of data. It aids the planner in the allocation of limited resources by posing critical questions such as: Should the research design include interviews, questionnaires, observation, analysis of records, or a combination of these or other techniques? Should the methods of data collection be highly structured? Should the study involve the use of a sampling technique? Should the analysis be quantitative or qualitative? (Phillips, 1966)

The basic steps in the planning and conduct of research are (Isaac, 1974) the following:

1. Identify the problem area.
2. Survey the literature relating to it.
3. Define the actual problem for investigation in clear, specific terms.
4. Formulate testable hypotheses and define the basic concepts and variables.
5. State the underlying assumptions that govern the interpretation of results.
6. Construct the research design to maximize internal and external validity.
   a. Selection of subjects.
   b. Control and/or manipulation of relevant variables.
   c. Establishment of criteria to evaluate outcomes.
   d. Instrumentation—selection or development of the criterion measures.
7. Specify the data collection procedures.
8. Select the data analysis methodology.
9. Execute the research plan.
10. Evaluate the results and draw conclusions.

These steps are actually specific procedures that overlap and in many instances can be implemented simultaneously. A planner should consider their application in every instance, because they will provide objective data and conclusions about current and proposed programs.

EVALUATION DESIGN PROCESS

The evaluation design process has five major steps (Waller and Scanlon, 1973).

1. Analysis of the decision-making system.
2. Analysis of the program's operations.
3. Development of possible evaluation designs.
4. Estimation of benefits and costs of design, and selection of the design to be implemented.
5. Scheduling the work.

Step 1

This step provides the criteria for deciding how much and what types of information to seek in the evaluation. At a minimum, the following factors should be specified:

1. The users of the information to be obtained.
2. The transfer mechanisms for disseminating information to the users.
3. The amount, type, and detail of data that the users will need for action.
4. The criteria to be used to estimate benefits.
5. The criteria to be used to estimate the level of confidence of the information to be produced.
6. The levels of confidence the users would require before acting upon the information.

Step 2

This step provides the framework for measurement and comparison of program operations. It must specify the following:

1. A characterization of the program and its environment, in terms of measurable factors.
2. The instruments required to measure program objectives, program activities, and costs.
3. The data sources for each measure.
4. The assumptions relating intended program activities to the program's goals.
5. The expected impact that would result from testing each assumption underlying the program.
6. The type of measurements and comparisons feasible, under current or anticipated program organization, to use in testing each underlying assumption.
7. The cost of obtaining data from each source.
8. The quality of data from each source.

Step 3

This step develops alternative evaluation designs. For *each* hypothesis (program assumption) that may be tested, the following factors must be specified:

1. The measurements required.
2. The data sources for those measurements.
3. The comparisons to be made.

4. The analytical techniques for making the comparisons.
5. The level of confidence provided by the design.
6. The cost of conducting the necessary work.
7. The type and volume of findings that the design can be expected to produce.

Step 4

This step estimates the costs and benefits of each candidate design by comparing the estimates developed in Step 3 with the criteria developed in Step 1. For each design, the following factors must be determined:

1. The total cost of funds and staff.
2. The cost of dissemination and utilization.
3. The total benefits if the design were to be implemented.
4. A rough schedule for executing the design.

Once these factors are determined, the options can be presented to policy officials so that *they can readily understand them and select the design* best suited to their value judgments.

Normally, this selection can be made without completing the fifth step — preparation of a schedule for conducting the evaluation. Even so, a rough schedule must be estimated for each design, since it is important to know whether the evaluation can be timed to mesh with program operations and decision needs. After the selection is made, the final design step is completed.

Step 5

This step establishes the operational plan for implementing the selected design. Factors to be specified are the following:

1. The schedule for data collection and processing.
2. The schedule for analysis.
3. The planned process for dissemination and utilization of results.

EXPERIMENTATION

Principles of experimental research provide the basis for estimating the amount and direction of program effects. Experimentation utilizes empirical tests of hypotheses in a manner that strives to exclude or correct extraneous influences, thus clearing the way for reasonable inferences concerning factors of significance. In basic outline, experimentation does the following:

1. Exposes an experimental group to the experimental treatment program that is the independent variable symbolized as **X**. An example of **X** might be stress training for law enforcement officers.
2. Does not expose the control group to the independent variable.
3. Compares both groups on the dependent variable, symbolized as **Y**. In keeping with the above example, the purpose of the experiment would be to evaluate the effect of stress training on field performance.

Through the use of quantitative and qualitative criteria, measurements of effectiveness, and methods of statistical analysis, research experimentation compares outcomes for the control and experimental groups that were randomly selected from a common population. Random selection means that each person in the population experienced an equal opportunity to be selected for either group. The experimental program (independent variable) is applied to the experimental group and withheld from the control group. Because subjects were assigned at random (or matched on relevant traits, then randomly assigned), the groups may be considered comparable and observed differences credited to the experimental program.

A primary concern of experimentation is to seek out possible causal relationships between significant variables. Thee relations are made to surface by subjecting the data to statistical tests of significance. From the findings, the administrator may infer with known degrees of confidence how **X** affects **Y**. For example, he will be able to estimate whether **X** causes or leads to **Y**, and, if so, with what frequency.

This description of experimentation, popularly considered as the scientific method, contains these core components: dependent variable, independent variable, careful ignoring of irrelevant variables, and careful control of other relevant variables. When properly conducted, it leads to the *if-then* statement (Figure V-6): that is, if this is the case, then that will happen. If frustration, then aggression. The *then* part of the statement houses the dependent variable, whose effects are dependent upon how the investigator manipulates the *if* (independent) variable (National Advisory Commission Report on Criminal Justice Standards and Goals, 1973).

Data can be used in many forms, but in experimentation it is reduced to numbers so that the mass of observations can be analyzed and evaluated. The

Independent	Dependent
if - - - - - - → (then)	
variable	variable

Figure V-6. Single variable experimental design.

rules selected to assign numbers to observations are the criteria that define the level of measurement, the numerical scale employed in the experiment, and the statistical operations used to analyze the data.

LEVELS OF MEASUREMENT

The four levels of measurement in their ascending order of power are the nominal, ordinal, interval, and ratio scales. The higher the level, the more information there is about the phenomenon. For this reason, investigators should strive to use the highest possible level of measurement in a given situation.

Administrators should possess a working knowledge of the properties and uses of the four levels of measurement. Briefly, they are as follows:

1. The nominal or classificatory scale refers to the simplest level where numbers are used to distinguish persons or traits. Example: Male-female; married-single. The essence of this scale is classification. There is no numerical value attached to the classificatory scales, and they do not represent a value or amount of anything. Nominal measurements rest on two rules: all members of a set are assigned the same number, and each set has a different number.

2. The ordinal scale should be used when the observations can be related and rank-ordered into possessing *greater than* or *less than* amounts of the attribute under study. This scale distinguishes one object from another and also tells whether the object contains more or less of the trait than other objects in the set. The scale provides no information on the amount of difference between objects. It also possesses no absolute quantities, nor equal intervals between the numbers. For example, because the numbers are equally spaced on the scale does not mean that the underlying properties they represent are equally spaced, also. Radical differences in correspondence may go undetected. The ordinal scale possesses no true zero point, so there is no way to detect when the object contains none of the property.

3. Interval scale refers to the level of measurement that should be used when the distance between any two numbers is equal and of known size. This scale possesses all characteristics of the nominal and ordinal scales, plus numerically equal distances. This means that equal distances on the scale depict equal distances in what is being measured.

4. The ratio scale is the most sophisticated level and one rarely attained by social research. It possesses all properties of the other scales, plus absolute zero at its point of origin. This addition enables application of all arithmetic operation to data.

The ratio scale is used for physical measurements such as length, time, and weight. With its absolute zero, statements of ratios are meaningful; for example, a six-inch line is twice as long as a three-inch line.

Some form of a ratio scale should be used when the investigator needs to state relationships between variables as products: for example, an individual's preference for a given event equals the product of its utility to the investigator and the expectation of its happening.

In the process of program evaluation, much time is devoted to observing. Observations supply the raw material for testing the hypotheses. The first step in reducing the mass of data into a format understandable by the human mind is to redefine the observations into a numerical form that can be handled statistically. This is done by the measurement method. The degree of information achieved is dependent on the level of measurement utilized.

Properties of the four levels are summarized by Figure V-7. Each ascending level contains properties of the lower levels, and the higher the level, the more information is available.

Scale	Properties	Examples
Nominal	Classification	Male–Female, True–False
Ordinal	Classification + order	H.S. grade level, height of individuals.
Interval	Classification + order + equal units	IQ Scores, Income in Dollars.
Ratio	Classification + order + equal units + absolute zero.	Can Add & Subtract Scores, Compare Scores.

Figure V-7. Properties of the four levels of measurement.

ISOMORPHISM

Measurement procedures should be isomorphic (similar in form) to the central features of the variables under study and to the practical world of the organization.

The most important choice and the first step in measurement procedures identifies what concepts to measure and then defines the activities that will set them in motion. This choice is critical, because many measurements can be meaningless: elaborate, precise techniques that define trivia are worse than useless because of wasted resources. How can this be avoided? By tying measurements to reality. That is, by actuating concepts, defining the rating scale, and defining the rules of correspondence so that the outcome—the measurements—reasonably connect variables to the lived-in world.

When this connection holds, the measurement process is isomorphic: that is, identity or similarity of form, which is the ultimate goal of the measurement procedure (National Advisory Commission Report on Criminal Justice Standards and Goals, 1973).

STEPS IN THE MEASUREMENT PROCESS

Any measurement process should include the following steps:

1. Determine the objective—the purpose of the program. Without clear objectives, it is impossible to set standards to evaluate performance.
2. Decide relevant factors. These are easy to define when dealing with physical systems; not so with social systems where evaluation routinely proceeds with limited information.
3. Select key indicators of factors; indicators that are quantifiable or in some way translatable to numerical ratings.
4. Select or construct (a) the measuring method and (b) the measuring unit. For example, in measuring police field performance, the measuring method might include completion of a five-point ordinal-scaled questionnaire by first line supervisors. The measuring unit is the quantity or amount of the concerned concept contained in the observation. This unit is usually fixed arbitrarily and standardized for all observations. In the example of field performance, after establishing a standard unit, the investigator would estimate how many units of, say, *initiative* were *expressed* by each subject.
5. Apply the measuring unit to the concept to be measured according to the preset rules of correspondence. This step starts the main action of measurement by translating the observation to a number (the number of units).
6. Examine the data with appropriate methods of statistical analysis.
7. Evaluate effectiveness of the measurement process by assessing its contributions to the program's objectives.

Measurement prescribes certain processes involving an observer, an observation, and some form of measuring instrument, the combination of which produces a number (the measure) that stands for the observation. The overall process follows certain requirements decided initially and set forth in the research design (National Advisory Commission on Criminal Justice Standards and Goals, 1973).

RESEARCH INSTRUMENTS

Data collection instruments should portray systematic and standardized procedures for obtaining information. They are extensions of measurement theory in that they serve the technical purpose of translating variables into numbers.

Categorized by their degree of directness, the main instruments and techniques include interviews, questionnaires, direct observations, participant observations, analysis of records, and projective techniques.

When drafting an interview or questionnaire schedule, the following criteria should guide selection of its contents:

1. Is the question akin to the research problem? Except for identifying data, all items should elicit information that can be used to test the hypotheses.
2. Is the question appropriate? Some inquiries need an unstructured, open-ended question such as opinions, intentions, and attitudes. Others can be collected by concise closed questions such as the choice between alternative events.
3. Is the question loaded, does it suggest an answer? These questions threaten validity. Example: Asking whether a person visited the police department during their last open house may receive many *false positive* replies because of the question's high degree of social desirability (National Advisory Commission on Criminal Justice Standards and Goals, 1973).
4. Does the question ask for information that the respondent does not possess? To offset this absence, *information filter* questions should be used. That is, describe the thrust of the question before asking for an opinion. Example: describing a new method to expedite court cases before asking for a value judgment.
5. Is the question weighted with social desirability? People tend to answer in ways that enhance their self-image, and may respond with what they think they should believe rather than what they do.
6. Questions that call for personal information should be posed after rapport is established.
7. Are the questions clear? To aid clarity, the questioner should: limit each question to one idea; avoid ambiguous expressions, long questions, and words with double meanings; pose the question in a clear context, unless ambiguity is used deliberately to draw out different viewpoints; specify the time, place, and context the respondent is expected to assume; preface unfamiliar or complicated questions with an explanatory paragraph or illustrations; and recount the question according to the respondent's experience rather than in generalities.

The sequence and administration of schedules can strongly sway answers. The following guidelines should be considered when designing the instrument:

1. For a given topic, begin with a general question followed by more specific ones. This harmonizes with the funnel technique of leading off with broad open-ended inquiries, then narrowing down to specifics.
2. The order should be logical and avoid abrupt transition in issues. Possible orderings: easy to difficult; chronological; general to specific; special locations for sensitive questions; or random locations to eliminate researcher bias.
3. Questions about controversial issues may antagonize the respondent and taint all subsequent answers. These should be dealt with last.
4. All schedules should be pretested for clarity and validity on a group similar to the research sample.
5. Some questions should be repeated to build in measures of reliability. If the person answers a question one way at the beginning and another way later on, the question may not be reliable.
6. Avoid initial questions that disclose the purpose of the research. In trying to be helpful, the subject may sacrifice candor.
7. The schedule should be reviewed by persons knowledgeable about the research problem (National Advisory Commission on Criminal Justice Standards and Goals, 1973).

A relatively simple questionnaire is shown in Figure V-8. Such an instrument can be of extreme importance to judges, because studies show that jurors' attitudes are formed largely by the efficiency and orderliness with which their time has been used and their treatment by all officials with whom they come in contact. A judge's actions, especially in showing appreciation for jurors' time, can have a profound influence on their view of the court (National Institute of Law Enforcement and Criminal Justice, 1974).

OBSERVATION

Observation is the oldest technique for collecting data. It is handy when observing a particular situation or event or when individuals do not choose to talk

1. Data should be recorded as it occurs.
2. To escape the volumes of data that accompany ambiguity of purpose, observations should address specific issues.
3. Observations apply to overt actions only. They should not be used to evaluate personal perceptions such as beliefs, values, and feelings.

Observer bias is something that a planner must monitor in social research. Techniques to reduce bias include the following (Simons, 1969):

1. Train the observers.
2. Specify the observers' tasks as closely as possible.

Your answers to the following questions will help improve jury service. All responses are voluntary and confidential.

1. Approximately how many hours did you spend at the courthouse? _____

2. Of these hours in the courthouse, what percent was spent in the jury waiting room? _____

3. How many times were you chosen to report to a courtroom for the jury selection process? _____

4. How many times were you actually selected to be a juror? _____

5. Have you ever served on jury duty before? _____ How many times? _____

6. How would you rate the following factors? (Answer all)

		Good	Adequate	Poor
A.	Initial orientation	☐	☐	☐
B.	Treatment by court personnel	☐	☐	☐
C.	Physical comforts	☐	☐	☐
D.	Personal safety	☐	☐	☐
E.	Parking facilities	☐	☐	☐
F.	Eating facilities	☐	☐	☐
G.	Scheduling of your time	☐	☐	☐

7. Did you lose income as a result of jury service?   ☐ Yes

                                                      ☐ No

8. After having served, what is your impression of jury service? (Answer one)

A. The same as before — favorable? ☐
B. The same as before — unfavorable? ☐
C. More favorable than before? ☐
D. Less favorable than before? ☐

9. In what ways do you think jury service can be improved?

_____

_____

_____

The following information will help evaluate the results and responses to this questionnaire:

10. Age: 18-20   21-24   25-34   35-44   45-54   55-64   65-over
                ☐   ☐   ☐   ☐   ☐   ☐   ☐

11. Sex: ☐ Female
              ☐ Male

Figure V-8. Jury service exit questionnaire.

3. Require observers to refer frequently to detailed instructions.
4. Require immediate and detailed reporting whenever possible.
5. Use cameras and tape recorders when appropriate.
6. Have at least two people observe the same event.

INTERVIEWERS

Interviewers should be carefully selected and trained. Rewarding results depend on the skill as interviewers. Their screening should concentrate on at least the following criteria (National Advisory Commission Report on Standards and Goals, 1973):

1. Maturity, intelligence and poise. These traits encourage cooperation and contacts conducive to candid, truthful answers.
2. Ability to interact easily with people, communicate importance of the experiment, and gain cooperation.
3. Ability to perceive and record responses objectively.
4. Noncommittal, nonjudgmental attitude and demeanor.

A recent review of the literature on *interviewer effects* indicates that, with a few exceptions, variations in response to interviewers is trivial. The exceptions involve the interviewer characteristics of sex and race. Sudman and Bradburn suggest that there is some evidence that these characteristics matter when they are related to the topics covered by the survey. Even with these interviewer variabilities, the researchers have concluded that the quality of a survey depends on the interviewer's ability and not their personal characteristics (Alwin, 1978).

PARTICIPANT OBSERVERS

Participant observation has had limited application in criminal justice, but where it *has* been used, it reveals behavior that is seldom obtained by other research techniques.

Two researchers have distinguished among three types of participant observer roles (Phillips, 1966):

1. The investigator may be a member of the group being studied.
2. The researcher may join the group in the role of one who is there to observe.
3. The investigator may pose as a member although not.

Ethically, this process raises a question that must be answered prior to engaging in observation of this nature. Is it justifiable to conduct research in any group when those being observed are not aware of the status of the participant observer?

It is the judgment of the authors that participant observation should be severely limited in criminal justice. What if a crime is committed by a member of the group. Would it be reported? As a general rule, the perils of such research clearly exceeds the potential rewards.

Other methods are definitely preferable. The bottom line is that such a research technique is self cost-effective.

This chapter has introduced the planner to some basic considerations in data collection and analysis. This was accomplished by discussing data availability in the criminal justice system and briefly discussing the data requirements needed for criminal justice. Data collection and analysis considerations were presented, and consideration was given to levels of measurement and the classification of data collection.

In the next chapter, the reader is introduced to alternatives in management planning.

TOPICS FOR DISCUSSION

1. Discuss each of the three classifications of data collection.
2. Discuss how experimentation can be used in the criminal justice environment.
3. Discuss the steps in the measurement process.
4. Discuss the criteria used in guiding the selection of the content for a questionnaire.
5. Discuss the steps that should be taken in survey research. Explain their relevance to the scientific method.
6. List four criteria for the screening of interviewers.
7. Identify six techniques that can be used to reduce observer bias.
8. Compare and contrast the various roles of participant observers.

REFERENCES

Alwin, Duane F., editor, *Survey Design and Analysis.* Beverly Hills, 1978.

Anthony, Robert N. *Planning and Control Systems: A Framework for Analysis,* Harvard Business School, 1965.

Babbie, Earl. *The Practice of Social Research,* 3rd Ed. Belmont, CA.: Wadsworth, 1983.

Bailey, Kenneth. *Methods of Social Research.* New York: The Free Press: A Division of Macmillian Publishing Co., 1978.

Bureau of Justice Statistics. *Sourcebook of Criminal Justice Statistics.* Washington, D.C.: G.P.O., 1981.

Doleschal, Eugene. Sources of basic criminal justice statistics: A brief annotated guide with commentaries. *Criminal Justice Abstracts,* 8:11, 1979.

Francis, J. and F. Woodcock, *People at Work,* La Jolla, CA., University Associates, 1975.

Isaac, Stephen. *Handbook in Research and Evaluation.* San Diego: Robert R. Knapp, Publisher, 1974.

Law Enforcement Assistance Administration. *A Guide to Juror Usage*. Washington, D.C.: G.P.O., 1974.

National Advisory Commission on Criminal Justice Standards and Goals. *Criminal Justice System*. Washington, D.C.: G.P.O., 1973.

Phillips, Bernard. *Social Research*. New York: The Macmillan Co., 1966.

Price, Barbara, and Baunach, Phyllis (eds.). *Criminal Justice Research: New Models and Findings*. California: Sage Publications, 1980.

Robinson, Edward J. *Public Relations and Survey Research*. New York: Appleton-Century-Crofts, 1969.

Sanders, William and Pinhey, Thomas. *The Conduct of Social Research*. New York: CBS College Publishing, 1983.

Simon, Herbert. *A Framework for Decision Making*. Proceedings of a Symposium on Decision Theory, Athens, Ohio: Ohio University, 1963.

Simon, Julian L. *Basic Research Methods in Social Science*. New York: Random House, 1969.

Weidman, Donald, et al. *Intensive Evaluation for Criminal Justice Planning Agencies*. Washington, D.C.: G.P.O., 1975.

Chapter VI

ALTERNATIVES IN MANAGEMENT PLANNING

The objective of this step in the planning process is to identify systematically and select alternative problem-solving solutions. These solutions will be developed in direct response to the mission statements, goals, and objectives described in the previous chapters, and which were approved by policymakers. After solutions are identified, it then becomes necessary to select one or more that will best satisfy the prestated problems, objectives, available resources, and constraints. The identification and selection of solutions is a difficult task, and the planning process can only provide a structure for evaluating alternatives. Throughout this chapter, planning tools that can help organize one's thinking, searching, and selection are reviewed.

The first point in the development of alternative solutions is to examine the functions of each element of the criminal justice system and determine if, in any way, they can contribute significantly to the accomplishment of a given objective, goal, or program. The purpose of this effort is to encourage the consideration of all resources available and to insure the cooperation and coordination of the system components involved.

During this step, the initiative for the planning effort passes, in most cases, to the operating agencies within the system. This insures that those who will be responsible for implementing solutions help to determine what that solution will be. The planning staff and their policy advisors should, however, continue to provide direction and guidance by first identifying the components of the criminal justice system who may be involved in attaining a stated objective, then by establishing criteria for this selection among the alternatives, and finally by making available the resources for implementation for those alternatives that meet the selection criteria.

In Chapter II, the roles, responsibilities, and functions of each of the criminal justice system agencies were discussed in detail. Figure VI-1 presents a summary of those functions that will prove useful as responsibility for the identification of alternative solutions is assigned to each agency.

The breakdown of functions can vary, depending upon the level of planning and analysis. For example, if planning is being done for one agency within the system, the previously listed system components might

Component	Function
Law Enforcement	Detection
Police	Deterrence
Sheriff	Investigation
Private	Order Maintenance
State	Service
Federal	Prevention
Courts	Warrants
Prosecutor	Preliminary Hearings
Defender	Plea Bargaining
Public	Prosecution
Private	Defense
Magistrates	Trial
Judges	Sentencing
Corrections	Custody
Probation	Rehabilitation
Parole	Pre-Sentence Investigation
Institutional	Supervision
	Revocation
	Conditions of Parole
Community	Crisis Intervention
Health	Prevention
Social	Post Release Service
Recreation	Social Service
Education	
Unions	
Employers	
Action Groups	
Employment	

Figure VI-1. Functions of the justice system.

be the various departments or divisions within a given agency. The functions then, would describe the responsibility/capability of each department.

INVOLVEMENT MATRIX

One method for identifying the system components most likely to be involved in solving a particular problem through the accomplishment of specific goals and objectives is seen in Figure VI-2.

In this example, the problems, goals, and objectives are listed in priority order in the horizontal axis, while the system components are listed in the vertical axis, thus forming a matrix. Obviously there may be more than two problems or two goals, and/or two objectives for each goal. Planners build the matrix to fit the results of the particular problem identification and goal and objective-setting process. Then the boxes of the matrix must be marked, indicating which system component can contribute to the accomplishment

Problems / System Component	#1 PRIORITY PROBLEM				#2 PRIORITY PROBLEM			
	#1 Priority Goal		#2 Priority Goal		#1 Priority Goal		#2 Priority Goal	
	#1 Obj.	#2 Obj.	#1 Obj.	#2 Obj.	#1 Obj.	#2 Obj.	#1 Obj.	#2 Obj.
Law Enforcement a. Police	X					X	X	
b. Sheriff		X	X					
c. Other								
Courts a. Prosecutor	X	X		X	X	X	X	
b. Public Defender								
Corrections a. Probation					X			
b. Parole								
c. Institutional		X						
Community a. Health				X			X	
b. Social	X							
c. Educational						X		

Figure VI-2. System component involvement matrix.

of a stated objective. The resource each component can provide may be noted in each box.

To further illustrate this matrix, assume that the planning organization identified the following stated situation:

Problem: Dangerous drug and narcotic usage by juveniles is increasing at an alarming rate.

Goal: Reduce the use of dangerous drugs and narcotics by juveniles.

Objective: Reduce juvenile dangerous drugs and narcotics usage by 30 percent in 36 months.

Solution Project Under Consideration: Develop and conduct one countrywide educational program for youth on the hazards of narcotics and dangerous drug usage over a twelve month period.

Solution Project Expectation: Reduce the use of dangerous drugs and narcotics by juveniles 10 percent in 36 months. The matrix for this situation might then be as depicted in Figure VI-3.

In this example, the planners have indicated the primary manner in which each type of agency will most likely be involved (i.e., personnel and training, facilities and equipment, other) and the type of agency that should be responsible for coordinating planning efforts related to this objective. The method for determining the involvement of various organizations may be accomplished in a variety of ways but will generally depend on several considerations, including —

1. knowledge of causes underlying the problem, as demonstrated by previous studies and experience;
2. knowledge of the capabilities of the types of agencies involved;
3. relationship of the planning organization to the organizational components in terms of authority.

If this stage of the planning process is being conducted within a given system component agency rather than across multicomponent boundaries, the component column of the matrix just illustrated would contain the various departments, sections, or people within that component. The same analysis process would exist in relating the various departments to each of the problems, goals, and objectives.

SOLUTION DEVELOPMENT

At this point, the planner must get out of his ivory tower and down to his most persuasive and salesmanship-oriented personality. Each agency that has contributed to the achievement of an objective and that has been identified by the foregoing matrix must be contacted and sold on the idea of developing a solution. This task becomes progressively easier for the planner who has involved Criminal Justice people in problem solving, goal determination, objective identification, and formulation efforts. The salesmanship job is also easier when the planner can offer resource assistance; for example, grant funds and staff assistance in the development of projects. One word of caution, however — too much planning staff involvement in the development of agency projects results in a loss of commitment within that agency to assure that the project will be a success. Staff members will lose sight of being part of the project and feel it is being imposed from the outside.

PROBLEM GOAL, OBJECTIVE, SOLUTION, PROJECT EXPECT. SYSTEM COMPONENT	#1 PROBLEM JUVENILE USEAGE OF DRUGS AND NARCOTICS	
	#1 GOAL — Reduce Juvenile Drug and Narcotic Useage	
	#1 OBJECTIVE — Reduce Juvenile Drug and Narcotic Useage 30% in 36 months	
	SOLUTION/PROJECT A Develop & Conduct 1 County-wide Education Program in 12 Months	SOLUTION/PROJECT B Establish 3 Neighborhood Walk in Centers in 36 Months
	SOLUTION/PROJECT Expectation Reduce Juvenile Drug and Narcotic Useage 10% in 36 Months	SOLUTION/PROJECT Expectation Reduce Juvenile Drug and Narcotic Useage 10% in 36 Months
Law Enforcement		
a. Police	X Personnel & Training	
b. Sheriff	X Personnel & Training	
c. Other		
Courts		
a. Prosecutor		
b. Public Defender		
c. Courts		
d. Defense Attorney		
Corrections		
a. Probation	X Personnel & Training Develop Training for Other Agencies	
b. Institutional	X Personnel & Training Facilities & Equipment	
Community		
a. Education Agencies	X Personnel & Training Facilities & Equipment Primary Youth Contact	
b. Health Agencies	X Personnel & Training Expertise on Drug Effects	

Figure VI-3. Specific problem matrix.

Once there is a commitment of the system component to participate in and formulate a project to achieve an objective, the planner must be concerned with moving from the conceptual stage to implementation. At this point, the planner is looking for a word or phrase that tends to suggest a solution-oriented project concept. At this level of development, the researcher is not looking for a complete and detailed project description. For many crimes, the solution is quite evident. As in the juvenile drug education objective stated earlier, it is quite clear that establishing an education project and delivering specific juvenile education is needed.

Many times solution-oriented projects can be borrowed from other agencies with similar problems that have already implemented one or more solutions. One of the best resources for obtaining examples of projects that have been implemented elsewhere is the state planning agency (SPA). This source can provide examples of projects that have operated in a given state, and perhaps of projects within a specific region or county. Another source of information is through the National Institute of Justice — especially their publications on prescriptive packages and model programs (see Chapter V).

In addition to these sources of project suggestions, consideration may be given to some of the state and national professional trade journals associated with criminal justice agencies. They typically feature successful projects.

Last, but not least, *brainstorming* may be required. A conference is called of all those working on a problem (Mitchell, 1977). They meet to create ideas for its solution. All criticism is barred. Quantity of suggestions, rather than quality, is the aim. These last two factors contribute immediately to fruitful ideas, because both group and self-censure have been eliminated. A great many ideas produced in such a session may be foolish ideas and infeasible (for example, legalize crime). It is better to have twenty foolish ideas and ten good ones in a total of thirty than two foolish ones and three good ones in a total of five. Subsequent criticism can easily eliminate the foolishness, for competent criticism is easier to obtain than competent creativity.

The total output of such a group, where one person's idea may suggest something further to another individual, has been found more often than not to be greater than the total of the ideas advanced by the same number of people working in isolation.

When a list of ideas is produced, more ideas can usually be generated by taking combinations of those on the list. The potential is greater than merely the combination of all the pairs on the list.

In addition to just generating ideas, brainstorming can be used to create new solution-oriented concepts rather than relying on many somewhat overplayed and overimplemented solutions that have been, in the past, only partially successful.

At this point, many theoretical planners would challenge the foregoing concept of allowing the involved system components to generate their own solution or project ideas. The alternative, of course, would be for the planner to define a grand program to solve a problem. Then each component would simply be required to implement its portion of the program under the expert's direction. Unfortunately, in most cases, the state of the art in criminal justice planning is such that it is still in the developmental stage. Planners are not fully recognized as being an asset beyond a potential source for grant funds or a resource for accomplishing special nonrelated research activities. This is further complicated by the process nature of the nonsystem criminal justice system that was discussed in Chapter II. No one person or body of people, including planners, have authority to demand change from the criminal justice system. At best, the planner (through salesmanship) must *sell* recommendations to the system components and coordinate their efforts in implementing the recommendations. The result is that the shortest distance between two points (in this instance) is not necessarily a straight line, and the planner must become an expert in the art of compromise.

SELECTING THE BEST SOLUTION

As the subject of solution or project selection is approached, a further comment becomes appropriate. The process just completed (determining criminal justice system involvement and encouraging system components to develop solutions) may not be appropriate in some planning situations. Many times the criminal justice planner is confronted with a multitude of project solutions from all or a few of the criminal justice system agencies. It then becomes his job to recommend the best solution for implementation. However, the planner must be cautious not to *put all the eggs in one basket.* A balance of solutions for implementation from each of the system components must be found. Politicians and pressure groups can be a positive or negative influence on the decision-making process, but they can never be discounted. Project selection must always be evaluated in a political context. Another consideration is that outside funding might be available in one area and not in another. The planner should strive to balance the competing demands generated by internal and external sources.

Each of the solutions generated as project concepts or titles by the solution development effort must now be described in greater detail. The general format of this expanded description should include the following information:

1. Title of Project—the title should be descriptive, but limited to one or two lines.

2. Project Expectations—The expectations should describe the measurable results that the improvement is meant to accomplish; the expectation, quantification, and further definition of the related problem goal and objective statement.
3. Major Tasks to be accomplished—The general steps, or tasks, to be implemented to accomplish the previously stated expectations, should be described in detail.
4. Responsibilities—Organizational responsibility for the task activities should be clearly described. This may simply be the implementing agency or department, including the project director.
5. Resources—The resources (i.e., personnel, equipment, facilities) required must be identified; the availability of critical resources (i.e., key individuals, one-of-a-kind facilities) should be determined.
6. Budgets—Both the implementation and operational costs should be estimated; the estimates must distinguish between out-of-pocket costs and the prorated costs of existing resources. Typical budget expense categories used are—
   a. personal services;
   b. supplies and operations;
   c. travel/conferences;
   d. consultant services/construction;
   e. equipment.
7. Schedules—The elapsed time required to complete each task activity should be estimated. Measure from the date implementation is started.
8. Risk—Estimate potential risk that could result due to project failure. Intuitively estimate a percent figure of potential failure for each risk area identified.

The length of this expanded description should be three to five pages in length. Figure VI-4 illustrates a summary of a burglary crime prevention project.

This request for an expanded solution description is sometimes viewed by local agencies as the first step of the bureaucratic process, and may bring complaints about the paper work. It is better to spend time in drafting three to five papers prior to project activation than it would be to implement a project for thousands of dollars and ultimately find out it is not solving the problem.

Solution/Problem Analysis

As expanded solution descriptions are received from the components of the system, the first step in the selection analysis process is to identify those

1. TITLE: Burglary Crime Prevention

2. *Project Expectations:*
   a. Reduce reported burglaries at a level of 15% less than the 1975 reported rate per hundred thousand in 36 months.
   b. Increase burglary arrests by 10% over the 1975 arrest rate per hundred thousand in 36 months.
   c. Increase the burglary clearance rate by 10% over the 1975 clearance rate per hundred thousand in 36 months.
   d. Increase the value of stolen property recovered by 25% over the 1975 value in 36 months.

3. *Major Tasks To Be Accomplished:*

   Task A— Target Hardening
   Through the use of paid senior citizens contact each private residence, and concerned business in the city and perform facility security check. Mark and identify valuable property, and distribute burglary prevention literature.

   Task B—Improved Caseload Management
   After the completion of a case by case load study determine which cases have the greatest potential for being solved in priority of the available evidence and other relevant factors. Assign detective resources based upon these determined case priorities.

   Task C—Improved Crime Data Analysis
   Based upon past burglary statistics develop a predictive crime incidence model and allocate patrol and target hardening resources on a continual basis to the areas of the city exhibiting the greatest potential for burglaries as predicted by the model and officer experience.

Figure VI-4a. Project summary.

solutions which best address the highest priority-stated problems, goals, and objectives set forth by the policy people directing the planning organization. If the criminal justice system involvement activity has been used, this analysis will serve as a cross check to assure that the solutions that have been submitted still conform to the goals and objectives that the planning organization seeks to accomplish.

If solutions are solicited in a blanket fashion from all agencies, this analysis will be useful during initial screening in order to determine which of the proposed solutions are related to the accomplishments of the stated goal and objectives. A tool useful in performing this analysis is shown in Figure VI-5.

As the project expectation portion of the solution is read, the immediately foregoing matrix simply indicates which priority problem goal and objective is being addressed. The matrix will display those solutions that will implement the highest priority objectives and goals, thus solving the highest priority problems. From this example, it can be seen that solutions **A, B,** and **C** are preferable to solutions **D** and **E.** The first solutions are attempting to solve the number one priority problem; therefore, from analysis, solutions **D** and **E** could be eliminated. The cutoff point is subjective and can extend beyond the first problem, if resources permit.

4. *Responsibilities*

City of ———————————————————— Police Department,

Chief of Police ———————————————————— Project Director.

5. *Resources:*

Task A

Community senior citizen clubs, Police aids, student summer hirees, vibrator marking tools, crime prevention literature and premises security check training.

Task B

Consultant study services, detective training.

Task C

Consultant study services, limited off time computer services and patrol training.

6. *Budgets:*

Expenditure	Task A	Task B	Task C	Total
Personal Services	$20,000	$ 2,000	$ 2,000	$24,000
Consultant Services		10,000	10,000	20,000
Travel/Conferences	5,000			5,000
Supplies & Operation	5,000		5,000	10,000
Equipment	500			500
TOTAL	$30,500	$12,000	$17,000	$59,500

7. *Risk*

Task A

The result will probably be an increase in crimes reported initially. Also some difficulty might be experienced in getting the paid volunteers organized. 5% risk factor.

Task B

The major risk will be in convincing the detectives to follow the case investigation guidelines and priorities defined from the study. 5% risk factor.

Task C

The primary risk will be in the quality of historical data and in the assurance that the patrol division allocates its forces according to the crime predictions. 10% risk factor.

This project has an 80% potential for success or a 20% chance of failure.

Figure VI-4b.

Resource/Feasibility Analysis

The next step of the project selection consists of further expansion of the project descriptions that are most related to the high priority problem, goal, and objective areas, in order to determine their resource needs and their potential feasibility for success.

As stated in one planning guide (California Council on Criminal Justice, 1972):

> The criteria to be used in selecting among alternative improvements should be established by the policymakers of the planning organization and communicated to the organizational components involved. These criteria provide additional direction and guidance, improving the chances of acceptable and workable improvements being developed.

Solution \ Problem	#1 PRIORITY PROBLEM				#2 PRIORITY PROBLEM			
	#1 Priority Goal		#2 Priority Goal		#1 Priority Goal		#2 Priority Goal	
	#1 Obj.	#2 Obj.	#1 Obj.	#2 Obj.	#1 Obj.	#2 Obj.	#1 Obj.	#2 Obj.
SOLUTION/PROJECT #A	X			X				
SOLUTION/PROJECT #B	X	X	X					
SOLUTION/PROJECT #C	X	X	X	X				
SOLUTION/PROJECT #D					X		X	X
SOLUTION/PROJECT #E	X					X		

Figure VI-5. Problem solution analysis matrix.

The selection criteria are commonly grouped into two major categories. The first are resource requirements. Typical requirements are described as follows:

1. Financial — How much money is required to accomplish the solution? Which solution requires the least money?
2. Manpower — What are the manpower requirements needed to implement and operate the solution? Which project will use the least manpower? What is the dollar cost of the manpower needs?
3. Equipment — Are there special equipment needs that must be acquired to implement the solution? Which alternative requires the acquisition of the least amount of equipment? How much will the needed equipment cost?
4. Facilities — Are facilities available to house the solution operation? Which solution will require the least amount of additional funds? What will the facilities cost?
5. Knowledge — Does the system component responsible for the implementation of the solution have the *know-how* necessary to implement and operate the solution? How much will consultant services cost?
6. Time — How long will it take to accomplish the tasks? Which solution offers the quickest results?

Using a matrix similar to Figure VI-6, analysis can be made of each solution in view of each of the criteria. Since all of these criteria are equatable to dollars, except for time, which can be measured in months, use can be made of these as a common analysis measure. To complete the resource component, each of the solutions must be calculated in terms of dollar amounts or time and placed in descending rank order, seeking minimum amounts, and totaling the values for each solution. The solution with the smallest total would rank highest by this methodology.

Resource / Solution	FINANCIAL	MANPOWER	EQUIPMENT	FACILITIES	KNOWLEDGE	TIME	TOTAL RANKING
$ OR MO. SOLUTION A	180,000	103,200	6,000	10,800	30,000	36 MO.	
RANK	3	2	2	3	3	2	15
$ OR MO. SOLUTION B	135,000	103,800	4,000	7,200	20,000	24 MO.	
RANK	2	3	1	2	2	1	11
$ OR MO. SOLUTION C	36,000	32,000	4,000	0	0	48 MO.	
RANK	1	1	1	1	1	3	8

Figure VI-6. Resource matrix.

From the previous analysis, the best solution would be solution C with a rank score of eight. Second and third best would be solutions B and A, respectively.

The second major category of section criteria is feasibility. These criteria are typical as described below as follows:

1. Resource—The feasibility for obtaining the resources described above are considered. Generally, the fewer resources that are required, the easier they are to obtain.
2. Political—This takes into consideration the agency and community politics that would influence the implementation and operation of each solution.
3. Impact—Which solution will have the greatest impact in solving the prioritized problem, goals, and objectives.
4. Risk—Which alternative has the least amount of risk or greatest possibility for success in the accomplishment of its stated objective. A feel

for the risk factor can be obtained from the project summary, if the suggested format is used.

Again, using a matrix, one can analyze each solution in view of each of the above feasibility criteria. Unfortunately, there is no convenient means of quantifying the analysis measures. Therefore, one must rank each criteria subjectively, using one's best judgment. That is, in analyzing political feasibility between the solution alternatives, simply ask which of the alternatives is most politically feasible to implement and operate and then rate it with a number one. Then rate the next most politically feasible, and so on, with the remainder of the alternatives and criteria. To complete the feasibility matrix, total the individual ratings for each solution. The solution with the lowest rating is the most feasible, according to this analysis teahnique. The use of the feasibility analysis matrix is illustrated in Figure VI-7.

Feasibility / Solution	RESOURCE	POLITICAL	IMPACT	RISK	TOTAL RANKING
SOLUTION A	3	2	1	1	7
SOLUTION B	2	3	2	2	9
SOLUTION C	1	1	3	3	8

Figure VI-7. Feasibility analysis matrix.

From the above matrix, the most feasible solution is **A**, with a rank score of seven. Second and third best would be solutions **C** and **B**, respectively.

Summary Analysis

In order to complete the solution analysis and arrive at a solution-oriented project recommendation, the information gathered from the solution/problem analysis matrix, the resource analysis matrix, and the feasibility analysis must be brought together and viewed in totality. The relative importance of the results from the foregoing matrix analysis should be indicated. The purpose is to produce a numerical indicator, or weight, that conveys the combined judgment of those responsible for selecting among the alternative solutions. Generally, the weight assigned to the matrix analysis data will be subjective and meaningful only in relation to other criteria and for that situation.

In the example shown in Figure VI-8, the solution/problem analysis matrix data is approximately six times as important as the feasibility analysis data. Because of the nature of the resource analysis data, it is three times as important as the feasibility data and only half as important as the solution/problem data.

Solution Matrix Analysis Data	WEIGHT FACTOR	SOLUTION A	SOLUTION B	SOLUTION C
SOLUTION PROBLEM ANALYSIS	0.6X	3=1.8	2=1.2	1=0.6
RESOURCE ANALYSIS	0.3X	3=0.9	2=0.6	1=0.3
FEASIBILITY ANALYSIS	0.1X	2=0.2	1=0.1	3=0.3
TOTAL	1.0	2.9	1.9	1.2

Figure VI-8. Summary analysis matrix.

As an illustration, three matrix analysis data components have been scored in Figure VI-8. For each section criterion, the following scores were assigned to show the degree of alternative desirability: (1) the most, (2) second most, and (3) the least. This assignment of scores was based on the combined judgment of those responsible for selecting among alternatives. Once the scores have been assigned, the weighted scores are determined. Based on the total weighted scores in the example, Solution C is preferred, followed by Solution B and, finally, Solution A.

The final selection of the solution alternative is generally performed by the policymakers. Throughout this suggested project selection process, it is not the use of the various matrixes that is important; rather, it is the logical thought process that is employed. It is a process that insures the consideration of high priority problems, an assessment of resources, and an analysis of feasibility of project implementation.

SYSTEM IMPACT

With the selection of the preferred alternatives, the planning effort has defined how it intends to go about solving the major problems it faces. By the conclusion of this step, the major elements of the comprehensive criminal justice plan may have been completed. However, further planning is required in order to assure that those projects to be implemented do not create more problems than they cure elsewhere in the system.

Without the use of overly sophisticated and complex criminal justice system computer models, it is almost impossible to predict accurately the impact of any crime-reducing activity or criminal justice system improvement planning. However, a quick and simple method is available for projects designed to impact arrests or diversions from the system. This method can be employed with data typically available from state crime statistics offices.

As an example, assume that the executive officer of a Sheriff's Office of a medium-size county creates a county narcotics bureau whose objective is to increase felony drug arrests of nonuser/sellers by 150 during the upcoming year. If one uses a criminal justice system flow chart, as illustrated in Figure VI-9, and inserts in each box the most recent calendar year arrest and disposition base data available, one can project quantity and percent changes for each of the boxes shown.

In the base year there were 2,915 felony arrests. Five percent were released, 2.5 percent were transferred to other jurisdictions, 91 percent resulted in felony complaints, and 1.5 percent were filed as misdemeanors. If the county narcotics bureau had been implemented in the base year, and if its personnel reached the objective of 150 felony arrests, then the felony arrest figure would have been 3065. This means that instead of 152 people being released, 159 would have been released, if the assumption can be made that 5 percent of total arrests remains constant. If this same analysis is carried out for the remainder of the boxes in the flow chart, the planner can get a feel for the quantity and percent change impact that a project may have. The next step, then, is for the planner to contact each element in the system and forewarn them of the potential change. For example, the district attorney might be contacted and questioned as to whether another 139 felony complaints filed per year can be handled with the present staff. The answer may be that another investigator or trial lawyer will need to be added. Similar responses may be received from the courts and corrections areas when they learn of their expected work load increase. This is planning ahead.

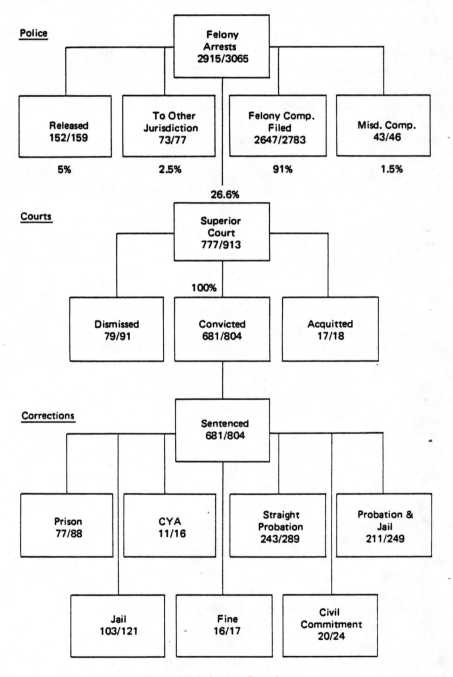

Figure VI-9. System flow chart.

Remember, however, this is a quick and simple analysis method. It is using old data and does not include current year felony arrest increases or decreases. It assumes that the percent relationship will remain constant and that the project will achieve its objective. It does not take into consideration that most of the project arrests will take place during the latter part of the project's first year, due to start-up activities. Even with all these threatening cautions, experience has indicated that this type of analysis can be within 95 percent to 98 percent accurate in predictions on a year-to-year basis using one-year-old base data. Obviously, the accuracy may change if the analysis is employed in high urban or small rural areas, because of the simple impact of crime volumes on percentages over a very large or very small service population.

The same approach can be used on diversion projects. In this instance, the impact will be more on the sentencing agencies or courts, depending upon where the diversion process takes place. If a new flow chart is developed for juvenile justice system projects, increasing arrests of juveniles or increasing juvenile diversion from the system can be assessed for system impact.

In this chapter, a format was set forth for the consideration and identification of the best solution. There is nothing magical about using the matrix as an analysis process; rather, it is the logical and systematic thinking that goes into filling in the matrix that forces the user to consider each criteria equally in view of each alternative being considered. Even the criteria suggested in this chapter for each of the matrices need not be the only criteria to be considered. It is illustrative of the types of factors that should be considered.

In the next chapter the preferred solution (as herein discussed) is implemented.

TOPICS FOR DISCUSSION

1. Discuss the importance of having each element of the criminal justice system participate in problem solving.
2. One of the best methods of identifying solution alternatives is to see what other agencies with similar problems have implemented as projects. Identify the hazards of relying solely on this method as a source for generating solutions.
3. Discuss the matrix technique in the selection of the best solution.
4. Discuss the criminal justice planner as a salesman.
5. Distinguish between the responsibilities of the planner and the policymaker during the project selection process.
6. Discuss the importance of assessing the impact of a given solution before it is implemented.
7. Discuss the simple system impact evaluation technique.

REFERENCES

A Guide for Criminal Justice Planning. Sacramento, California: Council on Criminal Justice (unpublished), 1971.

Cook, Thomas J., and Johnson, Ronald W. *Measuring Court Performance.* Research Triangle Park, North Carolina: Research Triangle Institute, 1981.

Connor, Patrick E. *Dimensions in Modern Management.* Boston: Houghton Mifflin Co., 1974.

Hall, Arthur D. *A Methodology for Systems Engineering.* New Jersey: D. Van Nostrand Company, Inc., 1962.

Howlett, Fred, and Hurst, Hunter. A systems approach to comprehensive criminal justice planning. *Crime and Delinquency, 18*:4, 1971.

Lynch, Ronald. *The Police Manager.* Boston: Holbrook Press, 1975.

Mitchel, Arnold. *Handbook of Forecasting Techniques.* Menlo Park, California: S.R.I., 1977.

Robin, Gerald D. *Introduction to the Criminal Justice System.* Cambridge, Harper and Row, Publishers, 1980.

Short, Ernest H., and Doolittle, Charles. *Records Management.* Washington, D.C.: G.P.O., July 1979.

Skoler, Daniel L. *Criminal Justice Organization, Financing, and Structure: Essays and Explorations.* Washington, D.C.: G.P.O., June 1978.

Chapter VII

IMPLEMENTATION PLANNING

Once the decision has been made to proceed with a preferred solution alternative, a more detailed plan for implementation must be developed. Implementation is the process of turning plans into action. Hence, the plan for implementation should provide for the development of the following:

1. An Implementation Strategy
2. A Work Plan
3. Reporting and Evaluation Plan

The plan for implementation should provide the coordination, control, and evaluation of the planned activities. The success of planning is largely determined by the success of these implemented improvements. The relationship of the requirements of implementation planning to the preceding steps is discussed by the following.

IMPLEMENTATION STRATEGY

The initial task in preparing for implementation is the statement of the strategy to be employed in the implementation of the solution alternative. Strategy defines the framework for effecting the plan. The project summary developed as part of the selection process can now be used as the framework for building this implementation plan and for presenting questions that need to be answered as part of the implementation strategy. The areas to be described, in terms of strategy, include—

1. agreement of project expectations;
2. organizational responsibilities and relationships;
3. general deployment of resources;
4. operational constraints;
5. potential problems.

In many cases, these elements will have been developed in earlier steps. However, the information developed previously should be reviewed and restated as necessary to develop a clear, consistent statement of implementation strategy. Only by this means can the commitment and expectations of the parties involved in the implementation of the solution be affirmed.

130

AGREEMENT OF OBJECTIVES

All parties to the implementation process need to sit down in a workshop environment and review the project's expectations and tasks as described in the expanded solution description. The individuals involved should include the project director,* the policy people to whom the director reports, and the people responsible for providing the project's resources.

The purpose of the workshop is for the project director to describe and interpret his understanding of each expectation and the tasks necessary to accomplish this expectation in detail to the rest of the participants. All parties involved should reach a "meeting of the minds" such that all are equally communicating and understanding exactly what is involved and expected from the project. Also, and equally important, each project participant should know exactly what is expected from him/her.

The format of this workshop session should be one of presentation by the project director and discussion and compromise solutions by the participants. If manpower or financing are not available to accomplish the stated tasks, now is the time to discover it and alter the task, objective, and/or project, as required to fit the resources actually available. If conflicts arise between the project director, the policymaker, and the resource provider, now is the time to get them resolved, or may they forever hold their peace.

ORGANIZATIONAL RESPONSIBILITIES AND RELATIONSHIPS

After the expectations and tasks are settled upon, the project director must delineate his organizational responsibilities and relationships with the policymakers and resource providers. The responsibilities and authority the project director can exercise with respect to resources should be carefully delineated, and the authority the project director can exercise in terms of day-to-day operational decisions or project changes must be clarified.

The responsibilities of the resource providers have to be understood and commitments made in order to insure completion of the project. The format for these discussions should be one of the project director stimulation followed by policymaker and resource provider discussion, compromise, and conclusion. The output should be a clearly understood set of guidelines indicating the roles, responsibilities, and authorities of all project participants.

---

*The title *project director* is used in this chapter to describe the person responsible for the day-to-day operation and management of the project.

GENERAL DEPLOYMENT OF RESOURCES

As the discussion of responsibilities and relationships is defined, the resource providers need to know when and where their resources will be required. The discussion of resource deployment will permit the project director and resource providers the opportunity to coordinate their activities and needs. The policymakers, on the other hand, are present to resolve any conflicts.

Techniques for deploying resources should be discussed and alternatives considered. The project director should be challenged on his recommendations. Generally, the project director becomes so immersed in the carrying out of the project that he loses sight of the fact that it may be a very small portion of the total activities in which the implementing agency is involved. Thus, priorities for the commitment of limited resources must be clearly understood by all parties. A community relations project activity for a police department is *small potatoes* compared to the crime fighting and emergency service responsibilities that the department must provide.

Conversely, however, the project director must make the policymakers aware when the project is being prioritized out of business. The project director must play the advocate role for the project and fight for its successful completion within commensurate authority and responsibility. It is most definitely a responsibility to alert the policymakers when resources are insufficient to meet the project's expectations.

OPERATIONAL CONSTRAINTS

The policymaker must clearly define the boundaries and rules under which the project can operate. The project director must know exactly what can or cannot be done.

Many of these operational constraints are already documented agency policy and should only be changed if their compliance may hamper project activities. This is especially true of covert apprehension and detection projects as alternatives to incarceration projects.

It is the project director's responsibility to become thoroughly familiar with fiscal and equipment constraints imposed by any agency from which the funds are received. The use of grant funds demands that the project director become thoroughly familiar with the fiscal affairs manual that serves as a monetary "bible." The primary failure of projects occurs in the accounting for monies in the prescribed manner. Unfortunately, common sense and honesty are not always sufficient. Accountants are included to set rules, and auditors like to catch people violating the rules.

POTENTIAL PROBLEMS

If participants can complete the foregoing discussions without identifying problems, they are not getting deep enough into the project activities. As problems arise, they should be discussed and potential solutions outlined.

Project director contact with similar projects implemented in other jurisdictions will also be helpful. Their experience and advice can be invaluable and should be actively sought. At this stage of the project's development, forewarning of future problems can lead to early and easy solutions.

As can be seen from the previous discussion on implementation strategy meetings, the project director must do a lot of prior preparation before confronting the policymakers and resource providers with strategy questions. The work plan and evaluation plan described in the remainder of this chapter should be completed before the implementation strategy meeting is attempted. These two plans will provide a focal point for meeting discussions and decisions. After the implementation strategy meeting, the project director will have a "design freeze," and the two plans can be updated.

WORK PLAN

The first step in the development of a work plan is the appointment of a project director who will have responsibility for organizing and implementing the project. Hall (1968) has stated:

> Sometimes he is called the project coordinator to emphasize one of his main functions. He serves as the center of communication on all matters among all the participants, and he is the point of contact with the persons responsible for the provision of the project resources. He allocates the manpower and budget resources to get the project done. (p. 128)

The actual rank or position of the project director is of little concern but needs to be a person who can turn plans into action. The project director must also possess verbal and written communicative skills as well as a thorough understanding of budgetary and scheduling processes. Equally important, the project director must be a persuader and compromiser who is goal oriented. Seldom having the sources to get a job done, reliance must, rather, be placed on ability to convince those persons who control the resources to expend them for the project.

It cannot be overly emphasized that the selection of a qualified project director does more for the potential success of a project than any other single factor.

PROJECT LIFE CYCLE

To better understand the development of a work plan, a brief description of a project's life cycle is useful. Figure VII-1 illustrates a project life cycle.

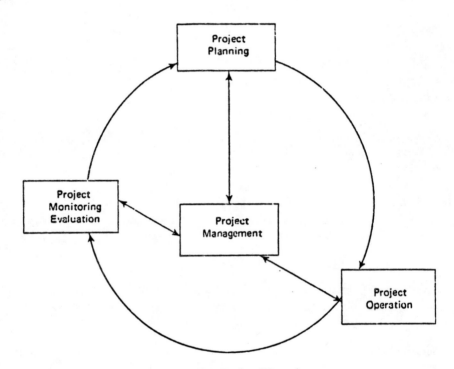

Figure VII-1. Project life cycle.

Project planning has to do with the preliminary preparation necessary to assure that the project can be implemented. It usually includes work plan development, task development, and budget and schedule preparation. Project implementation is simply the actual operation of the project tasks and activities. Project monitoring and evaluation is the policing of the project activities to assure that the tasks and activities are being accomplished as planned. Project management is the function of coordinating the entire project activities to assure that the project is accomplished. It includes the allocation and provision of resources and the day-to-day decision making to assure smooth project operation.

WORK PLAN

With this background of the proper selection of a project director and the understanding of a project life cycle, work plan preparation can commence. The purpose of the work plan is to organize the solution alternatives in a manner that will facilitate assignment of responsibility, coordination of effort among resources, and monitoring of costs, schedules, and results.

TASKS

The work effort necessary to carry out the planned project should be broken down into manageable, clearly defined work tasks. These tasks provide the basis for developing budgets, milestone schedules, and for assigning work responsibilities and resources. The development of tasks begins with the review of the problem, goals, objectives, and project expectations (see Figure VII-2). This structure is then expanded down to the level where work assignments can be made to specific organizational elements or individuals. Always two fundamental questions confront the project manager.

1. What work activities are necessary to accomplish the project expectations?
2. What is the output of this activity?

The number of subdivisions that will be created in the task breakdown structure depends on the size and complexity of the implementation effort and the number of participating organizations or individuals. Responsibility for the completion of task or subtask is assigned to a specific individual, group, department, or agency. In the example shown in Figure VII-2, Project Solution 1 (Develop and conduct one countywide educational program for youth in twelve months) consists of six major tasks. One of these major tasks (Develop instructional materials) has been further divided into three distinct subtasks. In a larger or more complicated project (i.e., development of a regional justice information system), additional levels of tasks would be required in order to specify work assignments for organizational elements or individuals.

As stated in "A Guide for Criminal Justice Planning" (California Council on Criminal Justice, 1971, p. 2–53):

> A complete description of work tasks does not automatically emerge at the beginning of implementation; it evolves through the life of an improvement as specific tasks are identified. As work proceeds, certain changes to the requirements inevitably develop. Since continuous updating of original plans is an essential part of an effective management control system, procedures must be established to facilitate this process without unduly burdening operating personnel.
>
> Responsibilities for the successful accomplishment of each work task should be

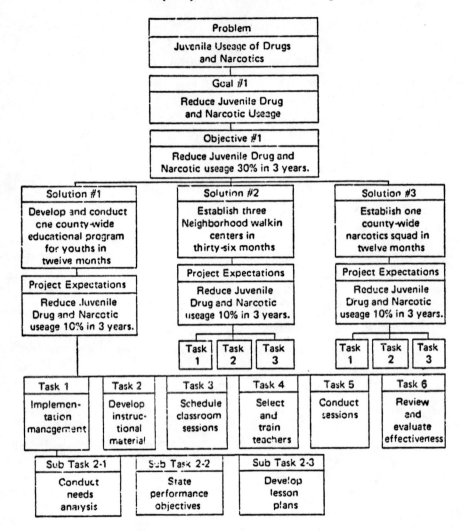

Figure VII-2. Task development.

assigned to specific organizational elements or individuals. These assignments should be based on the requirements of the tasks and the capabilities of the personnel involved.

Each work task must have a budget reflecting the total costs of the activities involved and an estimation of the time necessary to complete the task. A convenient way for gathering and organizing this information is illustrated in Figure VII-3. The method for gathering this budget data is for the project director to consult with each person or organization responsible for the completion of the task, and jointly estimate the costs and time necessary to accomplish the work. The example shown in Figure VII-3 reflects a budget breakdown for the tasks developed in Figure VII-2. The budget breakdown

Budget Category / Work Task	Personal Services $	Consultant Services $	Travel $	Equipment $	Supplies & Operating Expense $	Total $	Time to complete weeks
Task 1 Implementation Management	8,400	—	1,700	750	500	11,350	24 weeks
Task 2 Develop instructional material	—	30,000	—	—	—	30,000	9 weeks
Task 2-1 Conduct needs analysis	—	8,000	—	—	—	8,000	4 weeks
Task 2-2 State performance objectives	—	6,000	—	—	—	6,000	3 weeks
Task 2-3 Develop Lesson Plan	—	12,000	—	—	—	12,000	6 weeks
Task 3 Schedule classroom	700	—	—	1,500	—	2,200	2 weeks
Task 4 Select and train teachers	2,100	—	450	—	1,300	3,850	6 weeks
Task 5 Conduct Sessions	7,000	—	4,000	—	300	11,300	10 weeks
Task 6 Review & Evaluate	2,100	—	—	—	—	2,100	3 weeks

Figure VII-3. Task budgeting.

indicated a total project cost of $60,800 (the sum of each of the tasks 1 through 6). This example includes a consultant who will be paid $30,000 to accomplish subtasks 2-1, 2-2, and 2-3. The total project will be completed in 24 weeks, even though the sum of weeks for the individual tasks and subtasks is greater than 24 weeks. This is because many of the tasks are occurring at the same time. This is illustrated further in Figure VII-4.

Following are some suggestions for consideration in deriving estimates for each of the different budget categories. The actual location of individual cost items is, of course, dependent upon the rules, regulations, and/or guidelines of the resource providing the funding, but the following listed budgeting suggestions are typical of federal grant requirements:

1. Personal Service—List each position by title, and show the annual salary rate. If the person is employed part-time, list either the hourly rate and number of hours devoted to project (i.e., probation officer, $8/hour to $10/hour = $80); or the yearly salary and percentage of his working time devoted to the project (i.e., probation officer, $12,000/year × 50% = $6,000).

2. Employee Benefits—Indicate the percentage of the total cost of the benefits allowable to employees assigned to the project. Itemize each

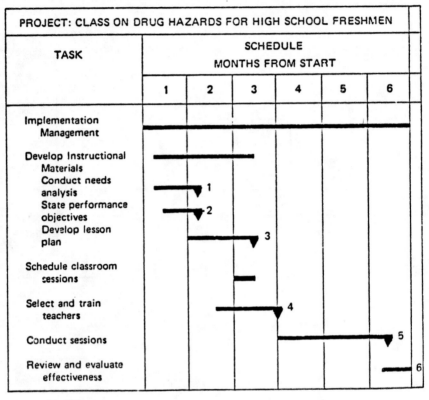

▼ = Milestone

Figure VII-4. A typical Gantt chart.

benefit by type and percentage (i.e., Public Employees Retirement System 2.8%).

3. Travel—Itemize travel expenses of project personnel by purpose, and show basis for computation (i.e., conference in San Francisco, 300 miles at 15¢/mile = $45; 2 days per diem @ $25/day = $50).

4. Consultant Services—List each type of consultant and the specific service to be rendered, the proposed fee rates per hour, and the total number of hours devoted to the project. For organizations, including professional organizations and educational institutions performing professional services, indicate the type of services being performed and the estimated contract price.

5. Equipment—Consider each type of item to be purchased and list separately with unit cost. Rented or leased equipment is typically budgeted as an operating expense. All installation costs included in the purchase of items of equipment are usually budgeted in the Equip-

ment category. The types of items to be considered as equipment are nonexpendable major items such as typewriters, desks, etc., consumable items, i.e. staplers and wastebaskets, are usually classified as expendable and are budgeted under supplies and operating expenses.

6. Supplies and Operating Expenses—List items within this category by major type (i.e., office supplies, training materials, research forms, equipment maintenance, equipment rental, telephone, and postage) and show basis for computation (x dollars per person for training materials, i.e., unusual supply items, special printing or mailings required for project). Actual rent or lease costs are budgeted in this category. Rented or leased equipment can be budgeted as an operating expense.

7. Total Project Cost—Itemize the category and task totals and enter in the appropriate box for each row and column.

MILESTONE SCHEDULES

Schedules define the duration and time sequence of project and task activities. Milestones identify major achievement points in the task activity. Typically, this is the expected product output completion date for a given task. Each work task must have a discrete beginning (start) and completion (stop) point separated by a relatively short time span.

Key schedule dates can be designated as milestones. Several types of dates might be chosen for use as milestones—

1. Delivery of a significant output (i.e., system design, final report);
2. Completion of a major task (i.e., develop instructional materials, select and train teachers);
3. Major decision point (i.e., shall we fund this improvement next year?).

A milestone generally occasions a formal review of the status of costs and schedules and the success of implementation.

The Gantt chart is a common method for displaying a detailed work plan. A representative portion of a Gantt chart is shown in VII-4.

The purpose of a Gantt chart is to provide the project director with a visual aid illustrating the time phasing and sequence of the various tasks associated with the project. Having this information, the director knows when and where to allocate resources to get the job done. It is known that one task must be complete before the beginning of another, if the second task requires the product of the first task before it can begin. Obviously, if the director wants to speed up the project, attempts should be made to run more tasks in parallel. This however, requires the use of more resources—especially manpower.

Special techniques exist that may provide assistance in the monitoring function as well as in scheduling work, allocating resources, and in controlling time and costs. These techniques, such as Program Evaluation and Review Techniques (PERT) and Critical-Path (CP), call for organizing the information from the Gantt chart into a network flow graph in which the nodes represent target dates and other events, and in which the branches represent activities. Using the methods prescribed by these techniques, the network may be analyzed for various purposes, such as to compute the probability that the task will be completed on schedule, or to locate the critical path through the network that prevents an earlier project completion date. Figure VII-5 is an example of a network diagram. For additional information on this technique, see chapter IV.

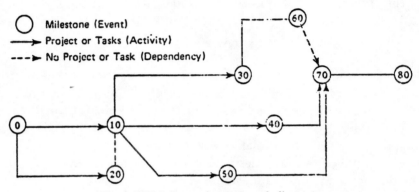

Figure VII-5. Example of network diagram.

REPORTING AND EVALUATION PLAN REPORTING

Reporting procedures must be planned to provide appropriate levels of management with necessary information to manage. This could mean detailed reports of accomplishment, schedules, and costs at the operating levels. At higher levels of management, reports that highlight progress are called for, but even then solely to the extent that the manager needs the information. Reports would normally cover the following aspects of implementation:

1. Evaluation of accomplishments
2. Monitoring of costs and schedules
3. Identification of problems
4. Discussion of corrective action taken/advised

The reporting system designed to meet the requirements described above should provide timely, understandable information, and should provide the basis for taking corrective actions. Monitoring of schedule and cost, for example, allows the following determinations to be made:

1. Work progress
2. Reasons for slippage
3. Need for additional resources
4. Need for technical assistance

EVALUATION

An essential activity in the planning process is the evaluation of the degree to which implemented improvements are meeting their objectives. Evaluation of accomplishment allows the following determinations to be made:

1. Contribution of the improvement to stated goals and objectives
2. Need for additional resources
3. Desirability of alternative approaches
4. Reasons for lack of success

The actual technique and methodologies for project evaluation are discussed in detail in the next chapter. The evaluation plan portion of the implementation plan described in this chapter refers to a plan for the allocation of project resources and activities to accomplish the selected evaluation methodology. The evaluation plan should contain (a complete discussion of the evaluation process is in Chapter VIII):

1. A description of the evaluation methodology to be used
2. Identification of the data that is to be collected
3. An indication as to who, how, and when the data is to be collected and analyzed
4. A summation of the project resources to accomplish the evaluation

This step concludes the description of the implementation planning process. In one sense, planning has been completed, and the responsibility for implementation and operation is passed to the hands of the operational staff.

In a larger sense, however, what has been described is but one cycle of a process that, once started, should be continuously in action. For one thing, problems do not appear according to a neat annual cycle; an organization cannot afford to restrict planning to a process that begins in the spring and ends the following winter.

Practical implementation planning seldom follows precisely the orderly steps that have been used in this chapter; major problems and constraints are all subject to change.

An example of what an implementation might contain is depicted in the following discussion of a Criminal Justice Education and Training Delivery System.

IMPLEMENTATION PLAN FOR AN
EDUCATION/TRAINING DELIVERY SYSTEM

The study is subdivided into four phases, each representing a segment of the project having an output requiring project task force review, operational input, and approval:

  I. Project Plan and Data Collection
  II. Analysis of Training/Education Needs and Considerations
  III. Resource Center Design
  IV. Implementation Plan

Phase I sets the stage for the study and subsequent decision making. The importance of having everyone aware of the consequences of the study and collecting the correct data becomes obvious in later phases. Phase I accomplishes the initial orientation of the task force, the definition of study parameters, the development of a detailed work plan, the development of a data collection and analysis plan, and the survey of each of the criminal justice departments. At the conclusion of the data collection task, the survey team and the task force will meet to review the data collection process and validate the findings and preliminary resource center system descriptions developed during this phase of the study.

Phase II identifies general and specific criminal justice education and training requirements. Phase II includes describing the existing training and education systems of the three counties within the region, performing an analysis, and evaluating the delivery of criminal justice training and education. Current and proposed operational needs will be identified and compared to current efforts and resources. Research will be made into other experiences having occurred elsewhere relative to an education and training resource center. This analysis and description of current training and education systems and requirements will be utilized to develop a set of preliminary system specifications for a resource center. These system requirements and specifications will then be presented to the task force for review and, upon concurrence, the project team will establish a final set of design criteria.

Based on the previous activities, the project can now confidently enter the design phase. During Phase III, we will develop a design for a resource center system that meets the immediate and long-range education and training needs, generates a program for developing manpower resources, and properly takes into account the external system interfaces with other institutions. This design will then be reviewed by the task force, and a finalized design will be established during a task force team design workshop.

These initial steps are to establish the roles of all the participants and to accomplish the orientation necessary to get the project off to a good start.

The acceptance of a final design for the criminal justice education/training system will be more likely if representatives of the departments participate in the development effort. It is recommended that the project task force act not only as a sounding board during the project, but also as an active participant in the analysis and design process. While not essential to the project, such project team participation in the design process could do much to ensure that the final work product is practical and useful.

A data-gathering system will be developed for the project. The system will define the process for carrying out the identification, collection, validation, and analysis of the project data. The process will involve the collection of all pertinent data directly from each criminal justice agency within the regions, as well as on-site surveys.

The emphasis of Phase IV is turning the agreed-upon resource system design into a plan for action.

Phase IV includes formulating an implementation plan and preparing the final report that will be used to sell the design. A plan will be developed for implementing the recommended center, including a grant proposal for funding. At the end of the project, a briefing of the project results will be presented to the task force.

It should be stressed that this approach requires strong involvement and input from representatives of the criminal justice agencies. In the long run, they are the users and must believe in the ultimate resource system. We have specified a number of points and specific tasks where criminal justice representatives are involved. In each of the four phases, there is active task force involvement. The remainder of this section discusses in detail the project task statements and methodology.

Phase I. Project Plan and Data Collection

Phase I is comprised of three tasks: finalizing a project plan, collecting relevant data from agencies and institutions in the regions as well as elsewhere in the state and nation, and preparing a description of the present delivery of criminal justice education and training. Phase I concludes with the review by the task force of the collected data and preliminary descriptions.

Task 1. Finalize Project Plan

The finalization of a project plan entails the accomplishment of five objectives —

1. Orienting Project Task Force Members;
2. Defining Study Parameters;
3. Developing a Data Collection/Analysis Plan;
4. Preparing a Detailed Work Plan.

The data collection plan will set forth a system for surveying the criminal justice agencies, academic institutions, and similar projects to determine current operational practices and system needs for education and training. The data collection/survey vehicle will be specifically designed for this project.

Task 2. Data Collection

The data collection will consist of surveys and interviews to define current practices, trends, and future education and training needs.

The data collection is broken down into three areas:

1. Operational Agency Survey
2. Education (Academic) Survey
3. Literature Search

OPERATIONAL AGENCY SURVEY

All agencies directly involved in or supportive of four counties' criminal justice systems will be surveyed, and the results of that survey will form the primary information base for this study. The survey will address such subject areas as curriculum, facilities, personnel, demand for the resource center, available resources, and in-house expertise. Following are data required to accomplish this survey; other areas may be included as they are identified by staff and task force members:

1. Determine all available preservice and in-service education and training resources in Regions J and M.
   a. The number of two-year, four-year, and university institutions within the region, and locations.
   b. Individual agency training programs (preperformance, in-service, and special programs).
2. Determine how many criminal justice personnel are in the regions by occupational level and component.
   a. Number of trainers within the regions, and by component.
3. Determine the level of training accomplished for each individual criminal justice employee.

a. POST training in the past three years for each of the criminal justice personnel.

b. Type and amount of training for each occupational level and component.

4. Determine the recruitment and selection standards for each agency in the regions for all criminal justice personnel.

   a. The entry level requirements for the criminal justice agencies.

5. Determine the staff turnover rate for each criminal justice agency.

6. Determine the expected organizational expansion for each agency in the next five years.

   a. The manpower need beyond present staffing for each agency within the regions.

7. Determine what provisions are made for criminal justice personnel in individual upgrading through education and training.

   a. Incentives provided by the agency to encourage personnel to achieve additional higher education levels or training.

8. Determine education and training resource gaps.

   a. Lower divisions, upper divisions, and graduate programs needed in the regions.

   b. Special program needs such as management courses, courses for training officers, etc. (Identify where they are needed.)

EDUCATIONAL (ACADEMIC) SURVEY

During this portion of the data collection, colleges and universities in the regions will be contacted and provided with information relative to the project objectives. Discussions will be held with those institutions indicating an interest in affiliation, and affiliation recommendations will be made based on several considerations, including mutual benefit, facilities, expertise, faculty, costs, and current college curriculum.

Substantial differences exist in the types and kinds of training and educational programs available to the members of each agency. The lengths of training periods, both at the entrance and advanced levels, differ drastically. Resources available to one agency are not available to or used by the others and, more often than not, are not even known to exist.

There are similar positions existing in two or more agencies of the criminal justice system. The position incumbents, despite their similarity of functions, seldom receive the same educational-training treatment after satisfaction of preemployment requirements.

This survey study will identify existing areas of training-education curriculum duplication, areas of mutual concern presently void of curriculum, new system needs in terms of curriculum (general criminal justice system knowledge may be one systemwide need), and existing curriculum that appears noncompatible or required in only one agency or system component.

The result of the education study will be curriculum recommendations relative to training-education of all criminal justice system personnel utilizing the resource center concept of network resources and maximum interaction. Curriculum recommendations will be reviewed by the task force and by others possessing expertise in particular system disciplines.

LITERATURE SEARCH

This portion of the data collection effort will focus on the experiences of other training-education resource centers. The specific information to be produced from this effort covers the following areas:

1. Centralized versus decentralized operation
2. Sources of funding
3. Affiliation
4. administration coordination
5. Project STAR
6. National Standards and Goals

The literature search will cover areas that presently have the resource center concept in operation. The anticipated centers to be contacted are located at the following geographic areas:

1. Issaquah, Washington
2. Honolulu, Hawaii
3. Independence, Missouri
4. New York, New York
5. Modesto, California
6. Oroville, California
7. Santa Barbara/Ventura, California

As the surveys are conducted, a set of preliminary education and training system descriptions will be developed to portray the survey team's understanding and perception of the current criminal justice requirements.

These surveys will result in an overview of the entire system and provide information relative to the objectives and operations of the various system components.

Further, an intensive study of the planning board's staff documents, planning board member and staff inputs, and personal interviews with the executives and staffs of agencies operating within the two regions will be added to the information base for the regional information-gathering effort. The information gleaned from these sources will be reviewed and discussed by the project staff and by experts in the various training-professional disciplines. Armed with this information, the task force can begin to draw logical conclusions regarding the existing types and levels of training and education in each component of the system, determine existing and future needs of component, and identify appropriate areas of mutual concern and interface. A series of recommendations can begin to be formulated relative to the resource center and the regional needs, including but not limited to consideration of such issues as centralization versus decentralization, administration, curriculum, personnel, funding, participation, etc.

Task 3. Project Task Force Review of Data Collection

At the conclusion of the data collection phase, the survey team and the project task force will meet to review the data collection process and initial description of current education and training systems and informational findings from the surveys. This meeting will include a general orientation followed by detailed discussions concerning the findings. At least a day should be set aside for this effort.

Phase II. Analysis of Training/Education Needs and Considerations

Phase II of the project will entail the systematic description and analysis of the existing training/education systems, the identification of user education and training requirements, the development of a preliminary set of criminal resource center specifications, a review of the descriptions and specifications by the project task force, and a project team design workshop to establish the specific design criteria and specifications of the education/training center.

Task 4. Analysis of Existing Systems

The information from the surveys of the criminal justice agencies and external agencies will be further analyzed to determine the nature, characteristics, and scope of the present education/training systems in the regions. The review and comments from the task force meeting, coupled with additional data where necessary, will form the basis of this analysis. Projections will be prepared providing data to assist in determining future needs.

Because of the variations in delivery services, training needs are separated from educational needs. This division may be arbitrary and unworkable. If so, this will become known during the course of the project.

The important aspect of this task is getting beyond what is presently being carried out into the area of user requirements. Training needs will be classified into various categories such as subject matter, repetitiveness, etc. These requirements must include resources necessary to meet the needs.

Task 5. Establish Preliminary Specifications for a Criminal Justice Resource Center

The information developed in Task will be translated into a set of preliminary specifications for a resource center concept. These specifications will identify training and education requirements and demands in terms of resources that would be required from a resource center. PSI will also look at feasible alternative designs that will meet the regions' needs in this task. These specifications cover administrative control, instructional services, and staffing.

Task 6. Task Force Workshops

The completion of Phase II involves an extensive review of the work done to date by the project task force and project team. The workshop will be divided into two parts: the first is the review and approval of resource center specifications, and the second is the formulation of criteria for the resource center design. The products of Phase II will be reviewed by the project team. Discrepancies will be identified and adjusted. Descriptions, requirements, and preliminary resource system specifications will be used to form a set of project design criteria that will guide staff in Phase III.

Phase III. Conceptual Resource Center Design

A criminal justice resource center design and recommended description will be constructed in Phase III. A workshop will be used to finalize the criminal justice resource center design.

Task 7. Resource Center Design

The success of the entire project rests with the completion of this task. The understanding of the resource system concept, local conditions, and other factors completed earlier in the project culminates in this task. The conceptual design is based on considerable in-depth analysis and requires substantial feedback from the ultimate users.

The beginning point in completing the resource center design is identifying and developing the various practical alternative designs. Some design will come about by the results of the Literature Search undertaken in Task 2. Other designs will be identified during work in the regions. Each of these alternatives will be developed in sufficient detail, to allow for critical review and evaluation. Particular emphasis will focus on facility requirements, organizational and operational requirements, and staffing requirements.

COST ANALYSIS

Each design alternative will be costed out for implementation and first-year operation of the resource center. Costs will be determined based on curriculum, facility, affiliation, personnel, administration, equipment recommendations, overhead, etc. These analyses include identifying possible cost savings by using existing facilities, etc. A part of the ultimate design will use these analyses.

A major effort of this task is determining funding sources. It would appear that the principal source of initial capital outlay would have to come from ADA and grants. Annual operating costs could be partially supported by federal funds for several years, but ultimately the state and participating agencies would be required to take over total funding. Another possibility that must be explored is the implication of Senate Bill (SB) 90, "Property Tax Relief Act of 1972," which has provisions for making subventions to local government agencies to carry out state programs.

Part of the funding problem is determining the manner in which local users would be obligated to support the final resource design. Assessment, quota, rates, and other methods will be identified and evaluated.

Task 8. Task Force Workshop

The task force team will be reassembled for a review of the various resource center designs. PSI will provide an in-depth explanation of the details of each alternative design. The task force will use the criteria developed in Task 6 to evaluate each alternative. Upon completion of this evaluation, a design workshop will be carried out to establish a final recommended system.

Phase IV. Implementation Plan and Final Report

The final phase of the project will produce details of the final resource system design, an implementation plan, and the final report. The final report will be designed to be used as a grant request for funding the resource center.

Task 9. Prepare Implementation Plan

The implementation plan, as conceived by the team, is an action plan. Included in the plan are the specific details of the regional criminal justice resource system, the specific requirements (organizational, procedural and content, manpower, and facilities and equipment), and schedule for implementing the system with accompanying costs. A separate section of the plan addresses the potential political and legal constraints and needs. The implementation plan will be the document used by the task force members to inform and obtain agreement from user agencies and various local government officials. The plan will contain the following sections:

ORGANIZATIONAL REQUIREMENTS

This section of the implementation plan will indicate the type of organizational structure the resource center will have. Specific points covered in this section include

1. organization structure and hierarchy
2. user advisory committee
3. educational institutions liaison
4. evaluation and control
5. support services

PROCEDURAL AND TRAINING/EDUCATION REQUIREMENTS

This section spells out procedures, methodology, and course description. Subjects covered under procedures and methodology include

1. scheduling
2. coordination
3. facility and equipment usage
4. instructional services
5. instructional methodology

Material under course description provides the foundation for the detailed curriculum content. Specific discussion will be provided for

1. training area needs
2. education area need
3. course objectives
4. course subject area
5. course sources and resources

This section will document the curriculum content of basic courses, advanced and refresher courses, integrated criminal justice courses, and specialized and technical courses.

MANPOWER REQUIREMENTS

This section delineates the staffing needed to operate the criminal justice resource center. The material covered in this section includes

1. Qualifications and selection criteria
2. Permanent/temporary staff
3. Community resources and availability
4. Evaluation

The important factors covered in developing manpower needs will have some documentation included in the previous section.

EQUIPMENT AND FACILITIES

The documentation of the physical facilities and equipment needed to operate the criminal justice resource center is an important factor. If the center is defined as an institution with the primary objective of providing instructional resources—teaching personnel, library, audio-visual equipment and material, consultants, etc.—for the use of criminal justice agencies at their locations, the physical facilities must be flexible. Perhaps a central facility location, with the use of an education/training van, would provide a centralized base with the added advantage of decentralized capability. Further, the type of equipment needed to accomplish this objective will be documented.

The next step in Task 9 is preparing the implementation specifics, including a time-phase schedule, a budget, and a listing of possible political and legal constraints. Along with this implementation plan, the criminal justice and government officials can begin to take steps to assure all activity is completed in a logical manner.

IMPLEMENTATION SCHEDULE

The importance of proper scheduling is obvious. This subtask will identify and describe each event in terms of its objectives, methodology, and resources needed for completion, and listing output products. The interrelationship between events will be clearly identified, along with the critical path necessary to accomplish implementation. The implementation schedule will be made part of the final report. It will be used in preparing a grant proposal.

IMPLEMENTATION COSTS

No plan is complete without knowledge of the costs involved. This information is vital for decision making, planning present expenditures, and preparing future budgets. Decisions made in previous tasks relative to funding will be incorporated in this plan. Among the cost figures will be

1. Facilities (new remodeling or whatever is necessary)
2. Capital outlay equipment
3. Supplies
4. Library and reference documents
5. Salaries
6. Operating expenses
7. Other costs

IDENTIFICATION OF POLITICAL AND LEGAL CONSIDERATIONS

This subtask will assist and smooth the way for implementation. The effect of this portion of the report is to uncover possible pitfalls that may cause implementation difficulty. The plan will document the possible political constraints which might have some impact. This will entail looking at

1. Agency-oriented constraints (people)
2. District/county/city relationships
3. Special district controls
4. Single municipal control

This subtask will also look at the various legal ramifications in the area of funding. This includes, but is not limited to

1. Federal Government (LEAA)
2. HEW

3. OCJP
4. Operational Agencies
5. Counties
6. POST
7. State Board of Education

Task 10. Prepare Final Report

This project will be culminated with a final report. This document will contain a statement of resource center requirements and specifications, a description of the recommended system, any applicable alternatives, and the implementation plan.

This task will culminate with a formal briefing and presentation to the project task force.

TOPICS FOR DISCUSSION

1. Discuss the importance of implementation strategy.
2. Briefly discuss the importance of a project director as a key person in the success of any project.
3. Discuss the project life cycle concept.
4. Draft a work plan for the burglary prevention project discussed in Chapter VI.
5. Distinguish between goals, objectives and project expectation.
6. Differentiate between a Gantt Chart and a PERT or Critical-Path Chart.
7. Why should the reporting and evaluation plan be prepared before the project is implemented?

REFERENCES

Adams, Thomas. *Criminal Justice Organization and Management.* Pacific Palisades, California: Goodyear Publishing Co., 1974.

A Guide for Criminal Justice Planning, a booklet produced by the California Council on Criminal Justice, 1971, 67 pp.

Ewing, David, editor. *Long Range Planning for Management.* New York: Harper and Row, 1972.

Goetz, Billy. *Management Planning and Control.* New York: McGraw Hill, 1949.

Hall, Arthur D. *A Methodology for Systems Engineering.* New Jersey: Van Nostrand Company, Inc., 1962, p. 456.

Rossi, Robert et al. *Agencies Working Together—A Guide to Coordination and Planning.* Beverly Hills, CA: Sage Publications, 1982.

Schoderbek, Peter, Kefalas, Asterios, and Schoderbek, Charles. *Management Systems: Conceptual Considerations.* Dallas, Texas: Business Publications, Inc., 1975.

Steiner, George. *Strategic Planning: What Every Manager Must Know.* New York: Free Press, 1979.

Sherman, Philip. *Strategic Planning for Technology Industries.* Reading, Mass: Addison-Wesley, 1982.

Chapter VIII

EVALUATION OF PLANS

Preapproval review and impact completion evaluation are crucial, but often overlooked, components of successful program management. The quality of these review/evaluation activities is of such importance that more and more managers are coming to realize the benefits to be derived from seeing that they are performed well.

Specifically, this chapter will address the question of what is the management process, particularly as it relates to evaluation in the criminal justice environment. It will also discuss the need for both preapproval review and impact completion evaluation as the crucial evaluation components related to the four discernable components, namely

1. setting goals and objectives
2. program planning
3. program control
4. impact completion evaluation

Most managers perform some type of program evaluation. What they would like to do is improve the use of evaluation as a management tool. The problem is that a certain mystique now surrounds the evaluation process — particularly in the public sector. This has been partly caused by university-trained academic-theoretical individuals. They were not familiar with real operational agency problems and typically used Student's T Tests, Fisher's F, and multiple linear regression as a means of communicating their evaluation of results. Evaluation is a word of many connotations. It stretches from value considerations to worker performance rating to complex analyses. The common feature, however, is judgment. The sophistication of the tools may vary, and the objectivity of the rater may be different, but in all cases, someone examines and weighs a phenomenon (person, thing, or event) against a standard (Weiss, 1972 p. 1).

Another problem with evaluation has been that the word itself has gained a certain negative connotation. This has occurred primarily because of fallout from some early evaluation projects in which emphasis was placed on finding fault with the concept of the program — after the fact — instead of evaluating whether the program achieved its stated objectives.

There is an urgent need to ensure a better understanding of the evaluation process by appropriate managers and operating personnel. Once this basic understanding has been achieved, it will be much less difficult to design and implement evaluation components as part of projects undertaken.

A publication on evaluation research in corrections (Cooper, 1975) suggests that evaluation be defined as "a procedure for ascertaining whether an event, process, or situation (real or conceptualized) is better than another. The procedure may include steps for measuring 'how much better' and for explaining the reasons for the difference."

This definition provides a good base for understanding impact-completion evaluation, but does not address the evaluation environment. The remainder of this chapter will attempt to shed light on evaluation as an integral part of the planning process.

COMPONENTS OF EVALUATION—SETTING GOALS AND OBJECTIVES

Each program begins as a concept of a desired result. Generally, the concept is expressed in very broad terms. It is the job of the manager to define, as clearly as possible, the specific goal. Examples of goals are—

1. reduce criminal justice processing time of offenders;
2. improve uptime of street maintenance vehicles;
3. decrease turnaround time in handling citizens' complaints.

The next step is to relate specific objectives to the goal. Generally, objectives should be more definitive statements of the goal. There are usually one or more objectives associated with each goal. The objectives, being more specific, provide the basis for establishing limits (response times, money, personnel levels, etc.) for the program. They also describe the benefits to be obtained.

Stated objectives also serve another important purpose. Objectives provide the logical departure point for developing measures of performance for evaluating program results (Cooper, 1975). Since objectives relate to program results, statistical measures of performance are similarly related to objectives. Examples of objectives are the following:

1. Primary Importance: Objective 1—Reduce the criminal justice processing time of offenders by ten days within the next year.
2. Secondary Importance: Objective 2—Increase the recovery rate of total dollar value loss in burglaries by 10% over last year's.

As can be seen by the above two examples, we have not even started to discuss programs for accomplishment of our objectives. It is also quite possible to have several primary objectives and several secondary objectives.

Each one must be articulated. Emphasis is placed on the managers' awareness of objectives and the priorities that should be assigned to them.

PROGRAM PLANNING

Once the goal(s) and objectives of a program have been defined, the next step is to express these goals and objectives in terms of the activities that must be taken to achieve the desired results. These activities are referred to as programs of action.

Each program can be defined in terms of one or more projects. A single project may be directed at achieving a specific objective, or several programs and/or projects may be designed to jointly serve one objective. In some cases a certain program may be directed at achieving more than one of the objectives. A problem in evaluation is "How do you isolate which program accomplished the objective?"

Program development is the basic planning step in the program management process. It defines the needed resources and assesses whether they are available in order to meet the required goal(s) and objectives.

When objectives and programs are merged into a model, the impetus for review and evaluation is clear. This is illustrated in Figure VIII-1.

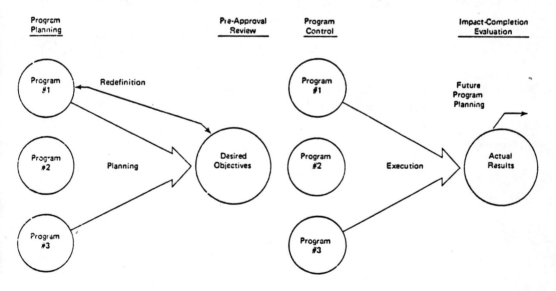

Figure VIII-1. Program planning review.

Preapproval review is the first half of the two-part review/evaluation process. As shown in Figure VIII-1, it is the last activity associated with the program planning process. Postcompletion evaluation, the last activity of the program execution process, is described later.

Preapproval review consists of the following basic activities:

1. Review (with the program team) the program's stated goal(s) and objectives for clarity and agreement.
2. Assess whether the real problem, or only its symptoms, have been defined.
3. Review the proposed program's structures.
4. Assess whether the proposed programs appear to be practical activities designed to achieve the stated goal(s) and objectives.
5. Review the work plans for the various programs.
6. Assess the feasibility of the work plans in terms of the manpower, money, materials, and time constraints involved.
7. Review the level of training and experience of program management in the basic techniques of program direction and control.
8. Assess whether a sufficient level of program management training and experiences exists to successfully guide this particular program.

There is one other element in the program planning process that has been deliberately left until last, in order to highlight it. This is the need for management to develop and agree on objective measures of performance by which the results of the program may be judged. Use of performance measures is the best way to implement the management-by-objectives concept in program management. Through the establishment of performance measures, management quantifies its goals and objectives in advance.

What is often missed is the fact that unless performance measures of criteria are set up and agreed to by the project team before a program begins, it is extremely difficult for the postcompletion evaluator to accurately audit the results. Of equal importance is another fact—unless the program manager agrees to these evaluation criteria before the program begins, the report of the postcompletion evaluation may be rejected by him as having missed the mark.

Performance measures are quantitative in nature and of three types—

1. Financial indicators;
2. Statistical (i.e., nonfinancial) indicators;
3. Milestone completion targets (time frame and tasks).

Program costs must be compared to the program budget on the account-by-account basis. The slippage of tasks completed could cause a program severe problems in terms of finances and completion.

The following are some examples of performance measures/criteria that have been used by project managers in conducting certain criminal justice projects:

1. Criminal justice agency feasibility
2. Costs
3. Time frame
4. Manpower required
5. Agency capability
6. Political feasibility
7. Ease of operation
8. Social feasibility

The *evaluation methodology* includes *techniques of* evaluation and answers the following four important questions:

1. *Who* will do the evaluation?
2. *When* will the evaluation take place?
3. *Where* will the evaluation take place?
4. *How* will the evaluation take place?

The first question necessitates a decision on whether the evaluation will be done by the agency, a consultant, etc. The second question poses the timing of the evaluation taking place: at the beginning of the program, continuously throughout the program, or at the end of the program. The third question deals with location of the evaluation effort. If it is done by an agency, will it be done by planning and research, school campus facility, or others? The fourth and last question deals with the specific technique of evaluation, namely, will one use a subjective questionnaire, computer analysis, or simple statistics collected? The criminal justice manager will probably not know the answers to these evaluation methodology questions, but he should be aware of them. They are endlessly recurring regardless of the nature of evaluation.

Management, therefore, must propose the criteria or performance measures with which it feels it would like to be judged in terms of successfully achieving a program's stated goals and objectives. The preapproval reviewer must independently assess whether he believes there are fair, relevant, and practical measures for use by the manager in guiding the program as well as the postcompletion evaluator in assessing results.

Preapproval review, which closes off the planning stage of a program, has a built-in feedback mechanism that must be satisfied before program execution can begin. If as a result of the review the manager feels weaknesses still exist in any of the areas appraised, recommendations should be made to the granting agency that the program team return to its planning mode and resubmit its program application.

The discussion thus far has only dealt with evaluating a *single program* against one or more *objectives* by a set of *criteria* utilizing a specific *evaluation methodology.* This evaluation scheme, as presented, does not assume existence of alternatives. If alternative programs exist, and this is common, one has to be able to determine which alternative program is most appropriate, thus, the need for prioritizing program selection.

In making a comparison, for example Programs **A** and **B**, it is absolutely *vital* to recognize that an accurate and meaningful evaluation is impossible if different criteria, evaluation methodologies, or objectives are used. Simply, Program **A** and Program **B** cannot be evaluated, one against the other, if objectives are changed or if different sets of criteria or evaluation methodologies are used. A simplistic guideline can be established in the evaluation for the purpose of comparing programs. Of the evaluation components (objectives, programs, criteria, and evaluation methodologies), *only program* may be varied; everything else must remain *constant.* In summary, programs cannot be compared if different objectives, criteria, and methodologies are used. A model for comparing two or more programs is depicted in Figure VIII-2.

When alternative programs are evaluated against the same objectives, using common criteria and the same evaluation methodology, a determination as to which program is the better of the alternatives is made by the use of two *factors.* Factor one is a simple determination as to which program *best meets* the objectives. The second factor deals with the criteria and how each program *measures up* against the criteria.

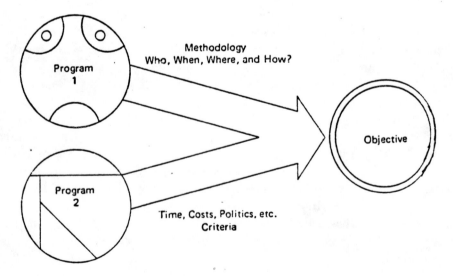

Figure VIII-2. Evaluation objective impact.

PROGRAM CONTROL

The program manager, having set goal(s) and objectives, established programs of action, undergone preapproval review, and received program funding, is now ready to energize the program. To assemble the designated program team, institute financial and administrative procedures, obtain facilities and supplies, and deposit program funds are necessary tasks.

During the execution phase, the manager's job is one of direction, coordination, and control. This is the stage when the highest use of interpersonal skills is made. One must monitor the use of resources according to plan, and hold frequent reviews to determine whether program activities are accomplishing desired results or whether certain activities (or indeed the entire program) must be altered to keep the program on track.

For assistance in this process, the manager needs a program control system. Such a system should include the following elements:

1. Budgetary control (i.e., financial plan or budget, periodic reporting of actual expenditures compared to budgeted amounts on an account-by-account and program-by-program basis, etc.)
2. Status reporting (i.e., periodic reporting of accomplishments according to the work plan and in terms of the preestablished measures of performance.)
3. Progress meetings (i.e., periodic meetings of the manager with the project staff to discuss progress in terms of the budget(s), work plan, and indicated performance.)

The most important aspect of program control is that it needs to be formalized. Seat-of-the-pants management may be an art, but consistently good results in program management are achieved by managers who utilize a structured approach based on modern management techniques.

The adequacy of the program control system in relation to the program it is designed to control is one of the important factors assessed in the preapproval review process.

IMPACT COMPLETION EVALUATION

After execution of the program is completed, the manager should evaluate results. Actually, if the program control system has been used properly, the postcompletion evaluation is merely the last in a series of similar program reviews to be conducted throughout the life of the program.

If the program control system has functioned properly, the manager knows on the last day of the program whether or not, according to expert judgment, the program has achieved its goal(s). In other words, at the close of the program, has each activity met the objectives established for the program?

Postcompletion evaluation for the manager, then, should actually be future-oriented in the sense that the manager should use this time to assess the knowledge received from the results achieved in terms of applicability to future programs.

There is another aspect to postcompletion evaluation, however; this is the second-level evaluation, which should be conducted by the same outside review-evaluation team that handled the preapproval review function. The reviewer (or review team) who conducted the preapproval review should now follow through and conduct the postcompletion evaluation.

It has been emphasized in the discussion thus far that if all the other planning and control steps of the program management process have been properly followed, postcompletion evaluation can be significantly reduced from its normal scope. This is chiefly because of the front-end review function built into the process at the preapproval review stage.

It also results from the fact that financial/statistical indicators of performance were established during the planning process so that the manager can now focus efforts during the postcompletion evaluation stage on whether reported results indicate that the expected goal(s) and objectives were achieved. What has happened all too frequently in the past is, the evaluator has had to make up criteria (many of which were subjective and qualitative in nature) after the fact. This is not only inefficient and time-consuming, it can also be counterproductive, if the manager of the program does not agree that the criteria selected accurately measure results.

The crucial elements of preapproval review and impact completion evaluation are the activities that harmonize the management process and provide the ultimate credibility to the success of the program. Often they constitute the crucial difference in successful program management, particularly in the case of programs funded with federal/state grants.

The above evaluation model has discussed the components of setting goals and objectives, program planning, program control, and impact-completion evaluation. It is well recognized that within each component, a complex set of interaction takes place. Many of these specific interactions, i.e. data collection and analysis, have been discussed in previous chapters.

The evaluation process should be viewed by the criminal justice manager as an integral part of the operation. A guide prepared under an LEAA grant (Evaluation in Criminal Justice Programs: Guidelines and Examples, 1973, p. 15) suggests that the managerial review should accommodate the following:

1. *Statement of Goals and Objectives:* Does the evaluation component offer a clear statement of the goals or objectives of the project? Goals or

objectives are simply summary statements highlighting what the project is designed to achieve. In order to be most useful, they should attempt to quantify desired results. As such, they provide the basis both for the evaluation planning and the evaluational analysis surrounding the project.

2. *Identification of Evaluation Measures:* Does the evaluation component clearly identify those measures appropriate to the project's stated goals or objectives? A project's goals or objectives are the key to the development of the overall evaluation component. Hence, the evaluation measures appropriate to a given project should correlate with the project's goals.

3. *Specification of Data Requirements:* Does the evaluation component exhaustively specify the data required for developing the evaluation measures? Data from a variety of sources and dealing with diverse aspects of a project will often be required to form a single evaluation measure. The specification of data requirements therefore, involves the explicit determination of the data elements required for the evaluation.

4. *Statement of Data Collection Approach:* Does the evaluation component state how the required data will be collected? Responsibility should be assigned for reporting various required data elements. Specific reporting periods ought to be established, and designs for simplified, standardized forms should be included.

5. *Statement of the Data Analysis Approach:* Does the evaluation component present a data analysis plan? The project goals or objectives and their associated evaluation measures must motivate any data analysis efforts. The analysis plan, then, should summarize how the data elements are to be combined to determine project results.

6. *Presentation of Evaluation Reporting Schedule:* Does the evaluation component present an appropriate evaluation reporting schedule both in terms of report content and timing? The successful results of programs are oftentimes determined by how well a manager performs his responsibilities for program evaluation.

An example evaluation design follows to practically describe for the reader how an evaluation design is structured.

Project Summary

Project Title: Special Case Processing for IMPACT Offenders

Project Objective: To reduce by 45 percent the amount of time it presently takes to process offenders charged with IMPACT crimes, from arrest through sentence.

This project proposes to improve the overall quality of justice within the adjudication process through procedural changes and supplemental personnel. This will include modifications in the entire process, from the municipal court arraignment through county court sentencing, and will stress three courts designated to hear only IMPACT offenders, decrease the present workload, and prepare the court system for the potential increase in arrests due to the implementation of other IMPACTs projects.

Project Description

The project proposes to establish an IMPACT–Crime Court process that will utilize select resources of the adjudication system to deal only with court cases involving IMPACT offenders. Specifically, additional prosecutors, public defenders, three judges, investigators, and clerks will be coordinated by an Assistant Court Administrator (reporting to the County Assignment Judge) for the purpose of reducing the amount of time it presently takes to process IMPACT offenders from arrest through sentence by 45 percent. Concurrently, it will attempt to reduce the process time for all offenders by 10 percent, and improve the overall quality of justice within the adjudication process.

These objectives will be pursued by modifying procedures and supplementing personnel in the existing courts system. These modifications will take place throughout the process (Municipal Court arraignment through county court sentencing) and will center around three existing courts designated to hear only IMPACT complaints.

Performance Objectives

1. To complete the adjudication process from arrest to sentencing offenders charged with IMPACT crimes within 90 days and as close to 60 days as possible (45% reduction over present time).
2. To achieve collateral benefits from the court process by arriving at a judicial determination in close proximity to the commission of the crime, thereby reducing the amount of rearrests prior to sentencing.
3. To achieve crime prevention benefits from the court process by arriving at a judicial determination in close proximity to the commission of the crime, thereby reducing the amount of rearrests prior to sentencing.
4. To improve the overall quality of justice within the judicial process.

Capability Objectives

1. To provide the municipal court the resources and supportive personnel necessary to rapidly process and refer complaints involving IMPACT crimes.
2. To provide the county courts the resources and supportive personnel necessary to complete the adjudication process through sentencing within ninety days.

Baseline Data

The Crime Analysis Team IMPACT target crime survey revealed that a definitive percentage of the total number of person-to-person target offenders were stranger-to-stranger. These percentages were applied to the number of complaints received by the Municipal Court (1982), complaints referred to the grand jury indictments returned to arrive at a projected case load level of 710. In tabular format

		Complaints (Arrests) Received By The Municipal Court	
All Offenses		*Stranger to Stranger**	
Murder	130	25	(19%)
Rape	178	103	(58%)
Robbery	1,337	976	(73%)
AA & B	1,379	427	(31%)
B & E	1,754	1754	(100%)
TOTALS	4,778	3285	

Complaints Referred To Grand Jury

All Offenses		*Stranger to Stranger*
Murder	111	21
Rape	130	75
Robbery	899	656
AA & B	894	277
B & E	523	523
TOTALS	2557	1552

		Indictments Returned (80% of Total County Figure)
All Offenses		*Stranger to Stranger*
Murder	62	12
Rape	53	31
Robbery	513	373
AA & B	222	69
B & E	225	225
TOTALS	1075	710

---

*Percentages taken from a survey of Impact offenses during a period from June 1981–May 1982

Current Timetable-Indicatable Offenses

The following narrative presents time (in court days) from an arrest to a sentencing for a typical indicatable offense under current conditions.

The municipal court is the first component of the judicial process to deal with the complaints in question. Arraignment is usually within twenty-four hours and usually, if the charge is substantiated, it will merely be referred to the prosecutor for presentation before the grand jury. Preliminary hearings, while taking place in less than 50 percent of the cases, must be considered, and usually take place seven days after arraignment.

10 days—Another day will be spent getting the complaint to the Prosecutor's office.

1 day—Another day will be spent once the complaint arrives at the Prosecutor's office in the normal course of sorting and redirecting the mail. Eventually it will be given to the pre-Grand Jury squad.

14 days—The pre-Grand Jury squad must prepare the cases for presentation to the Grand Jury. This requires obtaining arrest reports from the police department along with the follow-up reports, establishing witness lists, and drawing up subpoenas. Two weeks is required to accomplish this.

30 days—The present number of cases allowed for complaints that are ready for Grand Jury presentation, to be scheduled about one month ahead. During this one-month period, subpoenas are served by special Sheriff's squad.

7 days—If the Grand Jury returns an indictment, it will be presented to the Assignment Judge on the following Thursday. All indictments are presented on the same day, so some will have been returned in a shorter time than others, but a one-week delay is average.

7 days—The Criminal Court Clerk must schedule these cases for arraignment (pleading), and prepares notices of appearance. The arraignment date is usually set one week ahead. Pleas at arraignment are almost universally not guilty, so a trial date must be set. Also, at this time, defense counsel is usually formally assigned after court petition. Trials are usually scheduled about one week away.

40 days—Experience shows that many times defense cannot be prepared so rapidly, and along with various pretrial motions, forty days is actually required. If a defendant is found guilty, or if during this month a guilty plea is entered, a sentencing is done once a month, and another thirty days will be necessary till the case is finally disposed.

30 days—If a defendant is found guilty, or if during this month a guilty plea is entered, a sentencing day must be established. Since sentencing is done once a month, another thirty days will be necessary will the case is finally disposed.

It can be estimated, therefore, that present procedures allow for processing in around 139 days. Just as it is evident the courts alone are not responsible for this time lag, neither can the assignment of special courts to IMPACT offenses alone meet the stipulated objectives. Procedures also must be modified. The mechanism in its present form will not allow for a 60 to 90 day process.

Measures of Effectiveness

1. *Median* length of time in court days it takes IMPACT offender from arrest to sentencing.* The absolutely critical measure of effectiveness is the amount of time it takes the offender to be processed through the "IMPACT Court" process. A special reporting form has been developed that will document dates as well as the length of time (in court days) each step in the process takes. It is envisioned that the prosecuting attorney will complete each form (for each case he processes) and submit it to the project director after the sentencing date. The project director will be the focal point of the collection of these reporting forms and will clip off the names of the offenders (to assure confidentiality) when submitting the forms to IMPACT. Note that by employing such a reporting form, evaluators can pinpoint *where* delays, if any, are occurring in the system.
2. *Median length of time—other courts.* It is not clear at this time how this data will be procured. It is envisioned, however, that the project director will sample data available from the prosecutor's office to account for collateral time reduction benefits brought about by the implementation of special IMPACT courts.
3. *Number (%) of first offenders processed through the Court.* Number (%) of second, third, and so on, offenders processed through the court. While this measure has no direct bearing on the evaluation of time reduction benefits of this project, it is a critically important piece of data to collect. Such a measure will provide IMPACT evaluators with a current assessment of recidivism processed through the Court. This measure has important uses for the evaluation of other IMPACT projects, and hence will be collected here.
4. *The number (%) of target offenders processed through the Court who are rearrested before sentencing (by type of arrest).* The importance of this

---

*Median is utilized to discount the effects of an *outlier* value, i.e., one that is either so high or low as to make the average shift significantly one direction or the other.

measure is to account for any crime reduction benefits accrued to the speediness of the adjudication process; that is, does an inverse relationship exist between time spent in adjudication and the number of rearrests before sentencing? This data will emanate from two sources — the IMPACT Case Tracking system (described as follows) as well as a reporting form.

Measures of Efficiency

1. General
   a. The number (%) target offender cases placed on bail.
   b. The number (%) target offender cases placed in ROR status.
   c. The number (%) of target offender cases detained after arraignment.

   (all Monthly)

   d. The number (%) of target offender cases that involve individuals participating or previously participating in another IMPACT program.

   (Quarterly — estimate)

   The above three measures are important determinants in providing information as to how the system is operating. Item (c) is especially significant because it ties in with the IMPACT Case Tracking System described later. Since each IMPACT participant will be given a special IMPACT number, (and that will identify him to a particular program) careful accounting must be assured so that the participant is not given another IMPACT Number via the Court program. Only first offenders and non-IMPACT participants should receive IMPACT numbers via the Court program. ROR status will be subdivided by the type of program (if any) to which the defender has been diverted.

2. By Process
   a. Number of cases reviewed by Complaint and Indictment Section (monthly)
   b. Number of cases brought before Municipal Court arraignment (monthly)
   c. Number of cases for which there is a preliminary hearing (monthly)
   d. Number of cases presented to Grand Jury (monthly)
   e. Number of target offender cases where indictment by Grand Jury is sent down (monthly)
   f. Number of target offender cases where the Grand Jury presents no bills

g. Number of target offender cases assigned to each IMPACT Court (monthly)

h. Number of target offender pleadings (arraignment) "not guilty" before IMPACT judge (monthly)

i. Number of target offender "guilty" pleadings before IMPACT judge (monthly)

j. Document Sentencing for these guilty cases (special reporting format) — number of offenders in each sentencing alternative; median length of sentenced time

k. Number of target offender trials held (monthly)

l. Number of target offender guilty verdicts

m. Number of target offender not guilty verdicts

n. Number of guilty offenders times sentencing alternative

o. Median length of time for these sentences. The above fifteen measures will be gathered in the special reporting form and/or the IMPACT Performance Management System (PMS) reporting forms. They will be analyzed along various dimensions (example: comparison of the sentences of first versus second, third... offenders, number of indictments handed down by grand jury first versus second, third... offenders and so on).

3. Offender Data

a. Number of residents charged (special reporting form)

b. Number of offenders charged by type of IMPACT crime (forcible rape, robbery, atrocious assault and battery, and B & E) as well as a determination of the victim-offender relationship (special reporting form). The purpose of these measures is to provide an assessment of the type of cases (by crime) as well as the "source" of the offender. This latter data element is particularly important because it provides some indication of a crime displacement factor (nonresidents committing crime).

4. Additional Measures

a. Judges

b. Prosecutors

c. Public Defenders

One of the objectives of the project (and in some ways a constraint to speedy process) is to improve the overall quality of justice. Interviews developed by the CAT in conjunction with the Project Director will be conducted to gain some understanding of this element. The interviews, to occur at most every six months, will seek to discover

1. The relative quality of defense preparation;

2. The relative quality of prosecution's case;

   3. Satisfaction concerning pleas;
   4. Assessment of sentencing;
   5. The overall effectiveness of a special case processing concept.

Data Requirements

Utilizing a structured designation of **P** (primary), **S** (secondary), and **T** (tertiary), data elements would be classified as follows:

1. Number of court days arrest-sentencing IMPACT court (**P**—special reporting form, Prosecutor, Project Director, quarterly)*
2. Number of court days arrest—sentencing other courts (**P**—Prosecutor, Project Director, quarterly)
3. Number of first offenders processed through court, number of second, third—offenders processed through the Court (S, special reporting form, prosecutor, project director, assessed semiannually)
4. Number of offenders rearrested before sentencing (P, IMPACT Case Tracking, Special Reporting form, quarterly assessment)
5. Number of target offender cases placed on bail (S, PMS, monthly)
6. Number of target offender cases detained after arraignment (S, PMS, monthly)
7. Number of target offender cases involving IMPACT program participants (S, Special Reporting Form) (Note: all three will all be gathered via special reporting form)
8. Number of target offender cases ROR after arraignment (S, PMS)
9. Number of cases reviewed by Complaint and Indictment section (S, monthly, PMS)
10. Number of cases arraigned in municipal court (S, monthly, PMS)
11. Number of cases—preliminary hearing (S, monthly, PMS)
12. Number of cases presented to Grand Jury (S, monthly, PMS)
13. Number of cases where Grand Jury sends down indictment (S, monthly, PMS)
14. Number of cases where Grand Jury dismisses (S, monthly, PMS)
15. Number of cases assigned to each IMPACT judge (S, Quarterly, Special Reporting Form)
16. Number of cases pleading "guilty" before IMPACT judge (S, Quarterly, Special Reporting Form)
17. Number of offenders times sentence alternative, guilty pleadings (Semiannual Special reporting Form)
18. Number of months/offender sentenced after guilty pleading (Semiannual Special Reporting Form)

---

*Depends upon date of sentencing of particular case. Special reporting form cannot be submitted before then.

19. Number of trials (jury/nonjury) held per IMPACT court (S, Monthly, PMS)
20. Number of cases decided "guilty" (S, Special Reporting Form)
21. Number of cases decided "not guilty" (S, Special Reporting Form)
22. Number of guilty offenders times sentencing alternative, number of months/offender for these sentences (Special reporting format, assessed semiannually)
23. Number of residents charged
24. Number of offenders charged by type of IMPACT crime (special reporting form, assessed semiannually)

Data Constraints

Aside from potential problems in measuring the number of court days in other courts (non-IMPACT), there would seem to be no constraints in collecting data for this project.

Data Collection and Management

Data with respect to achievement of some performance and all capability objectives will be collected via the IMPACT PMS reporting system. Monthly reporting forms, with projections for the month matched against actual achievement, will be submitted to IMPACT for monitoring and analysis. When a report comes in for a particular reporting month, attached to it are the projections for the following month, and so on, for twelve operating months.

Management of PMS data will rest with the IMPACT Assistant Director for Police and Courts. Data reduction and analysis will be performed jointly by the assistant director and the IMPACT Evaluation Director.

Evaluation reports (to be issued quarterly) will be submitted through the IMPACT Director jointly by the CAT Evaluation Director and the Assistant Director for Police and Courts.

Data Validation

Validity as to the reporting of project monitor data to IMPACT will be assured by on-site visits by the CAT assistant director for Police and Courts (and any assistants he has to delegate that task).

Data utilized to evaluate performance objectives flow from reliable criminal justice agencies (Police and Courts); therefore, there are no plans to audit that data.

Evaluation Analysis

The essential thrust of the evaluation analysis is to assess the amount of time it takes an offender (consistent with maintaining a specified "quality of justice" level) from arrest to sentencing. This will be assessed via an aforementioned special reporting form. Supplementary analysis will include assessing general case load levels (by type of IMPACT crime) as well as various data dimensions, enumerated previously on the type of offenders processed.

Timing

The nature of the evaluation analysis (procuring data from special reporting forms) does not permit a regular quarterly assessment for data on the time it takes an offender to be processed. (The projected time is anywhere between 60 to 90 days). IMPACT will not receive this special reporting form until at least a week after sentence; therefore, it can be expected that an initial assessment of time would not be made until the middle of November 1983.

Impact Case Tracking—An Assessment of Recidivism

IMPACT is attempting to establish a system to track rehabilitative offenders as to their criminal activity after release from the project. The following will describe system operation.

Information concerning each participant will be gathered via an IMPACT Participant Profile form.

This form will be completed by the project director, and filed in the project's files. In addition, light blue 3 by 5 index cards containing "condensed" tracking information for each offender will be completed by the applicant (from the IMPACT Participant Profile form) and filed in alphabetical order by last name in the Police Department criminal history file. These cards are numbered consecutively and, as such, each participant is identified by his/her own number (called an "IMPACT Circular Number"). When an arrest report is filed, personnel must check the criminal history file (as a matter of course), and if the arrest report matches the IMPACT offender, a special report attached here will be filed to the IMPACT office. (Note: The special report will be mailed to IMPACT on a daily basis, regardless of whether an arrest occurs. This is to assure data accuracy).

For the Court Program, care must be taken not to complete a participant profile and a 3 by 5 index card (and therefore assign a name to a previous offender participating in an IMPACT program). (He or she will have a participant profile and a number already assigned)

The purpose here is to avoid duplication of numbers. "Recidivism" data will be aggregated on a monthly basis. To assure confidentiality, only the NPD and the project will have an awareness of who was arrested; IMPACT will possess only numbers and a master reference form indicating to which project that number belongs.

TOPICS FOR DISCUSSION

1. Discuss the importance of evaluation.
2. Describe the relationship of goals and objectives to the evaluation process.
3. Briefly describe program control.
4. Discuss the use of impact evaluation in criminal justice agencies.
5. Describe the steps necessary to prepare a viable evaluation component to a project or program.
6. Discuss the value of preapproval review to the evaluation process.

REFERENCES

Ackoff, Russel L. *Creating the Corporate Future: Plan or be Planned For.* New York: Wiley, 1981.

Ackoff, Russel L. Systems, organization and interdisciplinary research. In Donald P. Eckman, *Systems and Research and Design.* New York: John Wiley & Sons, 1961.

Adams, Stuart, *Evaluative Research in Corrections: A Practical Guide.* Law Enforcement Assistance Administration, Washington D.C.: U.S. Government Printing Office, March, 1975.

Alexander, Sidney. Income measurement in a dynamic economy. In W. T. Baxter and Signey Davidson, *Studies in Accounting Theory,* Homewood, Ill: Irwin, 1962.

Athey, Thomas H. *Systematic Systems Approach.* Englewood Cliffs, New Jersey: Prentice-Hall, 1982.

Carter, Robert. The evaluation of police programs. *The Police Chief,* November, 1971.

DeGreene, Kenyon. *The Adaptive Organization: Anticipation and Management of Crisis.* New York: Wiley, 1982.

Drucker, Peter F. *Management-Tasks, Responsibilities and Practices.* New York: Harper and Row, Publishers, 1973.

Emery, James C. *Organizational Planning and Control Systems.* New York: Macmillan, 1969.

Evaluation in Criminal Justice Programs: Guidelines and Examples, The Mitre Corporation, National IMPACT Program Evaluation, Law Enforcement Assistance Administration, Washington, D.C.: U. S. Government Printing Office, May, 1973.

Forrester, Jay W. Industrial dynamics—After the first decade. In William G. Scott, *Organizational Concepts and Analysis,* Belmont, Calif.: Dickinson, 1969.

Hughes, Charles L. *Goal Setting, Key to Individual and Organizational Effectiveness.* New York: American Management Association, 1965.

Katz, Daniel D. *The Social Psychology of Organizations.* New York: John Wiley & Sons, 1966.

McConkey, Dale D. *How to Manage by Results.* New York: American Management Association, 1965.

Miller, George A. The magical number seven, plus or minus two: Some limits on our capacity for processing information. *Psychological Review,* March 1956, No. 63.

Rossi, Peter, and Freeman, Howard. *Evaluation — A Systematic Approach,* 2nd edition. Beverly Hills, CA: Sage Pub., 1982.

Sayles, Leonard. *Managerial Behavior.* New York: McGraw Hill, 1964.

Scott, William, et al. *Organizational Theory: A Structural and Behavioral Analysis.* Homewood, IL: Irwin, 1981.

Simon, Herbert A. The architecture of complexity. *Proceedings American Philosophical Society,* December, 1962.

Suchman, Edward. *Evaluative Research.* New York: Russell Sage Foundation, 1967.

Weiss, Carol. *Evaluation Research, Methods of Assessing Program Effectiveness.* Englewood Cliffs, N.J.: Prentice-Hall, 1972.

Chapter IX

MANAGEMENT PLANNING

The process of management planning can be considered a framework or a set of organizational guidelines for the strategic planning process in criminal justice agencies. There is no single method applicable to all agencies. For example, a law enforcement agency must strategically plan (long-range — over three years) for the areas of staffing, manpower allocation, training, etc. Each agency has unique differences (e.g., management styles, community expectations) that require an agency to gauge their unique circumstances, which require the framework to be modified to match reality. This chapter will provide a management planning framework and examples that can be used in the development of strategic plans.

The primary approach is to conceptualize the criminal justice organization as a system that is composed of two basic subsystems: planning and control. Planning is an open-ended system that is followed by a control system. The control system closes the loop. It is within the control system that the management planning functions.

Expressed simply, organizational performance, in a management planning framework, is the comparison of actual performance against planned performance. This task requires two things to happen before it can be accomplished. Management must know what performance is desired and a mechanism must exist for measurement of that performance.

The *Standard College Dictionary* defines a system as an orderly combination or arrangement of parts into a whole, especially such combination according to some rational principle. Any number of similar definitions can be found in management literature.

From a management standpoint, the key aspect of a system is that it is composed on interacting parts (Ackoff, 1961). These parts in turn have subparts with parts and subparts being connected at interfaces that allow the output of one part of the system to become the input for another part.

Each component of the system transforms an input into an output. The relative cost of the transformation is a measure of the efficiency of the component, while the comparison of the output produced to the output desired is a measure of the effectiveness of the component. Whether the desired output serves the end purpose of the total system is a measure of

173

ability of the Criminal Justice Management planners to assign appropriate value goals.

The central requirement in a management planning context is the comparison of actual with planned behavior (Hughes, 1965). It is the step that closes the loop and provides the mechanism for adjustment and change. This is essentially an information feedback process and serves three important functions (Emery, 1969). First, it encourages realistic initial planning and goal formulation, decreasing the likelihood that blue sky, overzealous plans will appear publicly as future deviations to the plan. Second, effective evaluation guards against excessive deviation from the current plan, thereby decreasing the probability that one phase of an operation will cause a breakdown of overall coordination. Finally, it provides feedback for adaptive behavior. This information, it is hoped, should identify the source of the deviation so that adjustments can be made.

The criminal justice organization must assume that each division will take its goals seriously and attempt to meet the assigned requirements. A distinction, of course, must be made between the formal and the effective goals.

The stated goals adopted by the organization may or may not be the real ones. The real goals are those perceived by subordinates to be important. They are, to a great extent, determined by the evaluation and reward structure of the organization. A police chief may profess to be interested in quality, but if he bases promotions and awards on how quickly cases are processed, he should not be surprised if quality suffers. Thus, those areas which are evaluated are seen as objectives by the evaluated component, and behavior is likely to be directed toward meeting the established criteria in those areas (Drucker, 1973, Hunsicker, 1980).

An outline of the management-planning steps provides a framework for Criminal Justice agencies to follow. The steps are straightforward, information is exchanged as required, and decisions are made on a scheduled basis. The result is a rational development of a strategic management plan. These steps are

1. DEFINE AND ANALYZE THE PROBLEM
   Analyze the Organization. Consider: major problems, technology, community relations, service, manpower, finances, organization.
   Analyze the Environment. Consider: major problems, other Criminal Justice Agency interfaces, technology, socioeconomic factors.
2. FORECAST THE LONG RANGE
   Project the Future. Consider: Public service, personnel needs, socioeconomic factors.
3. SET OBJECTIVES AND GOALS
   Questions. Address the service your Criminal Justice Agency is in, what rate of service growth is satisfactory.

Define Mission and Operation of Your Criminal Justice Agency.
Set Objectives. Consider: current objective, technology alternatives, strengths and weaknesses, constraints, agency image.
Set Divisional Objectives.
Set Subobjectives.
Set Goals.

4. CONSIDER TECHNOLOGY
Consider Objectives for New Technology. Develop linkage between Agency objectives and technology.
Consider Risks. Assess level of risks of all programs.
Plan new Technology Development. Do a technology assessment; identify needs; identify time and resources needed.

5. ARTICULATE A STRATEGY
Identify Feasible Activities. Consider: current strategy, preplanning, critical factors, acceptable service levels, difference in desired and projected futures, trade-offs.
Select activities to be Implemented. Consider: Budget, priorities, evaluation procedures, ranking, selection, activities to be cancelled.
Do Contingency Planning. Develop alternative strategies for the possibility that assumptions may turn out to be wrong.

6. PREPARE THE PLAN
Allocate Resources. Project financial future, allocate resources in terms of personal services, operating expenses, capital outlay.
Develop Operational Plans. Consider: objectives, approach, resources, schedule.

7. SET MILESTONES AND RESPONSIBILITIES
Identify Specific Tasks. Include completion date with individuals who are responsible.

8. MONITOR PROGRESS
Compare Agency Progress to Plan. Modify as required.

This requires modification and adaptation before it can be used. It requires modification for particular situations as they occur in a variety of organizations' management styles.

How this framework might be used is best described through an example. Step 1 involves analyzing the organization and environment to assess problems and needs. The example chosen is quality of service in meeting citizen demands and requirements. This problem might be defined by the following scenario.

PROBLEM DEFINITION SCENARIO

The traditional perception of productivity measurement is usually perceived as relating inputs of a Criminal Justice service to the outputs. The outputs in Criminal Justice have been expressed as "arrest rates," "number of clients processed," "number of cases prosecuted," etc. These measurements tell us nothing about the quality of services provided. In Criminal Justice, the difficulty has been in defining and measuring service outputs in terms of effectiveness and efficiency. Service measurements need to be developed that provide Criminal Justice agencies with models of measuring efficiency and effectiveness in terms of quality of service in meeting citizen demands and requirements.

Past study efforts designed to provide new advancement in productivity measurement in government have fallen short in developing measures that are reliable, valid, understandable, transferable, and helpful in providing administrators with quantitative measures to select alternative delivery systems. Further, there has been limited efforts trying to relate population, economic, etc., factors with measurements of effectiveness (Urban Institute, 1972, PAR, 1972). The study efforts have not been able to bridge the expectation gap of academic research versus the need for implementable models for Criminal Justice services. The main limitation of these efforts is threefold, as follows:

1. They studied measures effecting only one agency, without looking for commonality and linkages of measures between service agencies.
2. They have neglected to explore measurement in terms of expectations from the public safety agency, the city administrator, and the general citizenry. The levels of effectiveness measures might vary drastically, depending upon the role each of the above plays in defining the mission of public safety delivery systems.
3. Past studies have been lacking with a plan for implementation into local government. Studies are still operating at the theoretical level instead of the practitioner's level.

The traditional measurement indicators of internal workload statistics have to be viewed as general indicators lacking any quality assessment. For example, in an emergency medical system, the patient is transported typically to an emergency hospital. To use reduction of response time as one indicator of effectiveness is absurd. One could reduce emergency medical response time by 20 percent and the patient is still dead on arrival. Therefore, it becomes critical to analyze the delivery system in light of the measurement. The case in point illustrates that a change in delivery of medical services by treating the patient at the scene would be a more meaningful alternative to delivery. The point is that in developing effectiveness measures, one has to be able to associate the measures with a particular delivery system. The delivery system may differ, depending on citizen need, city administrator need, or agency head need. This synthesis of factors is crucial to useful service measures.

The attributes of measurement criteria are—

1. in some aspects *quantifiable;*
2. designed to allow for *subjectivity* (Citizen perception);
3. constructed to allow local decision makers to *distinguish* among *alternative delivery systems;*
4. designed to be *understandable* and *transferable.*

Criminal Justice Agencies should consider constructing multiple optimization models to be used by local decision makers to measure service productivity and effectiveness.

To overcome problems of citizen needs and services in service goal formulation, agencies should conduct a stratification of citizen assessment for delivery services effectiveness. This stratification will correlate delivery service functions, i.e., police traffic control, with citizen requirements within the stratification, i.e., population density, mode of transportation—walk, drive, public transportation, etc. The stratification will determine service delivery requirements of each stratification.

The approach of formulating measurements, beyond statistics, victim surveys, etc., in developing optimizing models to determine delivery productivity and effectiveness is vital. The agencies and the public need this type of accountability to make decisions regarding scare resources.

The criminal justice agency could then carry forth with this problem by forecasting the long-range service expectations, setting goals and objectives, assessing how technology might impact future service delivery, develop and articulate a strategy, develop and prepare a plan, set milestones, and monitor the results. The point is that each agency will require some modification of this framework to their particular situation. However, a framework has provided the guidance and sequence of events to guide the agency in development of a meaningful strategic plan.

In summary, management planning should be thought of as a series of questions that must be addressed at each step of the planning process. Examples of these questions would be as follows:

Problems

1. What major problems is our agency currently facing?
2. What major problem is the agency likely to face over the next three to five years, or ten years?

3. What are the probable impacts of the problem's existence?
4. Has the agency faced the problem before?
5. What was done about it, and what were the results?
6. What are the possible solutions to the current and future problems?
7. What are the expected costs and benefits?
8. What are the major decisions that management must make?
9. What is behind the decision, e.g., why is it a major decision?
10. What are the alternatives that can be chosen?
11. What are the possible and probable outcomes of each of these choices?

Technological Capability

12. What is the status of our agencies' technologies in addressing the problems.
13. How is it used today?
14. How will we plan to use it?
15. What will be the status of each in the future?
16. What are our current program goals.
17. What service delivery changes are needed?
18. What is the quality of service provided as perceived by the public?
19. Is this satisfactory to the public?
20. Is this satisfactory to management?
21. How can it be improved?

Personnel

22. What personnel skills and technical expertise exist now in our agency?
23. What is the extent of these skills and expertise?
24. What skills and expertise are insufficient and in excess?
25. What are our plans for hiring of needed skills?
26. What training programs do we currently have?
27. Are these programs satisfactory?
28. What programs are planned?
29. How will these be implemented?

Resources

30. What is the current financial situation of our agency, city, county?
31. What will the future solvency of our government entity be?
32. How will this effect identified current and future problems?

Organization

33. How is the agency organized?
34. Why is it so organized?
35. What is the degree of centralization and/or divisional autonomy?
36. What are the advantages and disadvantages of the present organization structure?
37. What changes are reasonable to make?
38. What changes are planned to address current and future problems?
39. What benefits would result from these changes?

Management

40. What type of management does the agency have?
41. Is it formal, informal, dictatorial, relaxed, aggressive, risk taking, flexible, or other?
42. How else can top management be depicted?
43. What are the strengths and weaknesses of the agency's management?
44. What skills are strongest among our managers?
45. What skills are weakest?
46. What hiring plans have we?
47. What plans have we for replacement of managers in the future?
48. What training programs have we for managers?

The questions outlined are not meant to be all-inclusive but are meant to serve as a foundation for the management planning that needs to take place in criminal justice agencies.

Once a strategic management plan is completed, it is recommended that the following blockage questionnaire be administered to a selected sample of employees at all levels of the organization. Data collected can then be used to insure the successful implementation of the management plan (Francis and Woodcock, 1975):

Instructions

1. Use the Blockage Questionnaire Answer Sheet to respond to the statements.
2. Work through the statements, in numerical order, marking an "X" on the appropriate square of the grid if you think a statement about your organization is broadly true. If you think a statement is not broadly true, leave the square blank.

3. Do not spend a great deal of time considering each statement; a few seconds should be long enough.
4. Remember that the results will be worthwhile only if you are truthful.

Blockage Questionnaire

1. The department seems to recruit as many dullards as efficient people.
2. Lines of responsibility are unclear.
3. No one seems to have a clear understanding of what causes the department problems.
4. The organization is not short of skills, but they seem to be of the wrong kind.
5. It would help if people showed more interest in their jobs.
6. Good suggestions are not taken seriously.
7. Each major unit acts like a separate empire.
8. The managers (commanders) believe that people come to work only for money.
9. There are no clear successors to key people.
10. People do not spend adequate time planning for the future.
11. There is no central place where one can get all information about a case or person.
12. It takes too long for people to reach an acceptable standard of performance.
13. Jobs are not clearly defined.
14. There is not enough delegation.
15. Managers do not seem to have enough time to take training seriously.
16. There are no real incentives to improve performance, so people do not bother.
17. Unconventional ideas never get a hearing.
18. Groups do not get together and work on common problems.
19. Managers believe that tighter supervision produces increased results.
20. The organization often needs to hire new managers from the outside.
21. One of my major problems is that I do not know what is expected of me.
22. It takes a long time to get information from the originating source to those who need it.
23. The department has too few qualified civilians in technical positions.
24. The department reflects outdated standards and needs to be brought up to date.
25. Only top management participates in important decisions.
26. Units within the department have different attitudes on training— some take it seriously, others do not.

27. Punishments seem to be handed out more frequently than rewards.
28. The department would be more successful if more risks were taken.
29. People are not prepared to say what they really think.
30. Managers believe that people are basically lazy.
31. The department does not try to develop people for future positions.
32. Employees are told one thing and judged on another.
33. Valuable information is usually kept by individuals and rarely written down or shared.
34. Too many newcomers leave quickly.
35. Different parts of the department pull in different directions.
36. The department does not really know what talent is available.
37. Skills are picked up rather than learned systematically.
38. People are exploited—they are not rewarded adequately for the large amount of effort they exert.
39. Frequently, innovation is not rewarded.
40. In this department, it is every man for himself when the pressure is applied.
41. Managers would like to revert to the days when discipline reigned supreme.
42. Management does not identify and develop those who are potential high achievers.
43. Personal objectives have little in common with the department's aims.
44. There are too many duplicate records in the department.
45. Many employees are only barely efficient.
46. The executive has so much to do that it is impossible for the executive to keep in touch with everything.
47. The right information needed to make decisions is not readily available.
48. The managers had to learn the hard way and think others should do the same.
49. People in the organization do not really get a thorough explanation of how their performance is valued.
50. Other units/departments seem to have brighter ideas.
51. Each manager is responsible for his own unit and does not welcome interference.
52. The only reason this department exists is to satisfy lawmakers.
53. People do not know what the department has in mind for them in the future.
54. People are judged on personal characteristics rather than on their contributions.
55. Very little useful information is available for operational units.

56. There is resentment because new people seem to get the better jobs.
57. Some units within the department have more people than their contribution justifies.
58. The department operates on old ideas rather than on new ones.
59. Managers are not capable of training others.
60. If the chips were down, managers would not be fully prepared to extend themselves for the department.
61. Once something becomes an established practice, it is rarely challenged.
62. Meetings are not popular because they are generally unproductive.
63. Management does not care whether people are happy in their work.
64. Management succession and development cannot be planned; there are too many variables.
65. The department's future plans are of low quality.
66. There is too much effort devoted to producing useless statistical information.
67. There is really not much talent around.
68. All too often, important things either do not get done, or get done twice.
69. Labor turnover figures are not calculated.
70. Effectiveness could be increased if the right skills were available.
71. I do not feel supported in what I am trying to do.
72. This is a dynamic age, and the department is not moving fast enough.
73. Lessons learned in one unit of the department do not get transferred to others.
74. The department does not try to make jobs interesting and meaningful.
75. Many people are trained who later drop out.
76. Objectives are expressed in vague terms.
77. Records contain too many errors or are usually incomplete.
78. People with little or no talent and experience are hired.
79. Some managers are overloaded, while others have it easy.
80. Employees do not know how competitive the wages are because comparative figures are not available.
81. People are not encouraged to update their skills.
82. People do not get the opportunity to contribute, and as a result, do not feel committed.
83. People do not like to "rock the boat."
84. Competition inside the organization is so fierce that it becomes destructive.
85. Managers do not think that people are interested in the quality of their working lives.
86. The experience of senior managers is not wide enough.

87. Priorities are not clear.
88. There is no requirement for follow-up reports on open cases.
89. When recruiting, the department finds it difficult to sort out the wheat from the chaff.
90. There is no use talking about reorganization; attitudes are fixed.
91. Management-control information is not generated where it is needed.
92. Quality would be improved if the staff were more skilled.
93. The department pays below par, and people are dissatisfied.
94. Managers are not sufficiently responsive to changes in the external environment.
95. People could help each other more, but they do not seem to care.
96. Managers are not addressed by their first name.
97. Managers do not believe that management education has much to offer them.
98. Plans seem unreal.
99. Too little training is given new personnel on proper investigation and reporting techniques.
100. Whenever we have a new position identified, we usually get stuck with a person who cannot perform adequately.
101. Units within the department do not respect the work of other groups.
102. Management does not recognize the cost of a dissatisfied employee.
103. It is not surprising that newcomers sometimes receive a poor impression of the department, considering the way they are treated in the first few days.
104. People would welcome more challenge in their jobs.
105. Problems are not faced openly and frankly.
106. Teams do not consciously take steps to improve the way they work together.
107. There is a lot of under-the-surface fighting between managers.
108. Managers are not open about the future prospects of their people.
109. Decisions are made now that should have been made months ago.
110. I, personally, have a hard time finding information I need when I want it.

Blockage Questionnaire Answer Sheet

Follow the instructions given at the beginning of the questionnaire.

In the grid below, there are 110 squares, each one numbered to correspond to a question. Mark an "X" through the square if you think a statement about your organization is broadly true. If you think a statement is not broadly true, leave the square blank. Fill in the top lines first, working from left to right; then fill in the second line, etc. Be careful not to miss a question.

A	B	C	D	E	F	G	H	I	J	K
1	2	3	4	5	6	7	8	9	10	11
12	13	14	15	16	17	18	19	20	21	22
23	24	25	26	27	28	29	30	31	32	33
34	35	36	37	38	39	40	41	42	43	44
45	46	47	48	49	50	51	52	53	54	55
56	57	58	59	60	61	62	63	64	65	66
67	68	69	70	71	72	73	74	75	76	77
78	79	80	81	82	83	84	85	86	87	88
89	90	91	92	93	94	95	96	97	98	99
100	101	102	103	104	105	106	107	108	109	110

Total

When you have considered all 110 statements, total the number of "X's" in each vertical column.

Write below the total from each vertical column on the answer sheet.

Totals

A	
B	
C	
D	
E	
F	
G	
H	
I	
J	
K	

Blockage 1.   Inadequate Recruitment

Blockage 2.   Confused Organizational Structure

Blockage 3.   Inadequate Control

Blockage 4.   Poor Training

Blockage 5.   Low Motivation

Blockage 6.   Low Creativity

Blockage 7.   Poor Teamwork

Blockage 8.   Inappropriate Management Philosophy

Blockage 9.   Lack of Succession Planning and Management

Blockage 10.   Unclear Aims

Blockage 11.   Inadequate Information Systems

Blockages with the highest scores are those that need to be explored further.

Interpreting the Results

In Part One, we described the following eleven blockages to the effective use of people.

1. Inadequate Recruitment and Selection
2. Confused Organizational Structure
3. Inadequate Control
4. Poor Training
5. Low Motivation
6. Low Creativity
7. Poor Teamwork
8. Inappropriate Management Philosophy
9. Lack of Succession Planning and Management Development
10. Unclear Aims
11. Inadequate Information Systems

In the Blockage Questionnaire, you have been considering statements relating to these blockages. You can now arrive at your score for each blockage as it relates to your own organization.

Let us stress that the questionnaire has been designed only to give you an indication of where to start looking for the roots of your people problems. As such, it is not scientifically accurate, and the results will need further confirmation.

TOPICS FOR DISCUSSION

1. Define a strategic management plan.
2. Why is it important to understand the management planning framework?
3. Describe the important elements of the management planning framework.
4. Outline and explain the management planning steps. List several areas where these steps could be applied in a criminal justice agency.
5. Choose an organizational area that the management planning steps would be applicable, and describe how the steps would apply.

REFERENCES

Ackoff, Russell. Systems, organizations, and interdisciplinary research. In Donald P. Eckman, *Systems: Research and Design.* New York: John Wiley & Sons, 1961, pp. 26–42.

Athey, Thomas. *Systematic Systems Approach.* Englewood Cliffs, New Jersey: Prentice-Hall, 1982.

Drucker, Peter F. *Management: Task, Responsibilities and Practices.* New York: Harper & Row, 1973, p. 496.

Ebenstein, Michael and Krauss, J.: Strategic planning for information resource management. *Management Review,* New York: American Management Association, June, 1981, pp. 21–26.

Emery, James C. *Organizational Planning and Control Systems.* New York: MacMillan, 1969, pp. 140–142.

Hughes, Charles L. *Goals Setting, Key to Individual and Organizational Effectiveness.* New York: American Management Association, 1965, p. 158.

Hunsicker, Quincy, J. The malise of strategic planning. *Management Review,* New York: American Management Association, March, 1980, pp. 8–18.

Public Administration Review. Symposium on Productivity in Government, Nov/Dec., 1972.

Urban Institute/ICMA. *Improving Productivity Measurement and Evaluation for Local Government.* Washington, D.C., 1972.

Chapter X

OPERATIONAL PLANNING

Operational planning as defined here is the criminal justice agency planning needed to accomplish an objective from the present up to three years. This chapter will address areas that would be applicable to operational planning and provide a detailed example of how operational planning would take place, based upon an identified need in a particular problem area. An operational planning framework is presented that can be used by agencies in addressing operational planning problem areas.

OPERATIONAL PLANNING ENVIRONMENT

The operational planning environment covers numerous areas that agencies must address and develop plans for in effectively meeting their obligations. An operational plan might cover a particular problem; for example, a major parade in the city next weekend. It might address a particular crime; for example, an operational plan to curtail a burglary problem. It could encompass a plan for implementing a technology solution into the agency. The important aspect to operational planning (zero to three years) is not the area addressed but the planning discipline needed to effectively implement a workable solution. This chapter will address the planning needed by using an example and working through the steps involved in implementing the plan.

OPERATIONAL PLANNING FOR A
COMPUTER AIDED DISPATCH (CAD) SYSTEM

Clearly, there exists a definite need for law enforcement to think through the objectives, costs, planning, and preimplementation steps required to fully accept and utilize an operational CAD system.

The key operational planning considerations are the following:

1. Agencies should clarify the goals of the CAD system.
2. Agencies should carefully plan the implementation.
3. Agencies should clarify expectations and perceptions.
4. Agencies should be prepared to deal with change in the implementation of CAD systems.

5. Agencies should provide carefully planned and thought-out training programs.

STATEMENT OF PROBLEM–OPERATIONAL–PLANNING SCENARIO

As police organizations develop through time, they respond to task needs by creating methods for documenting incidents and events. Usually, this process is accomplished on a piecemeal basis without any overt effort to coordinate or evaluate source document development and/or processing procedures (such as complaint processing). Uncontrolled development has created unnecessary forms, duplication of effort, confused information flow, delays in response to citizen/officer requests for assistance, collection of unneeded information, and loss of needed data for task-related decision making.

An extensive amount of planning must be performed before police agencies make a commitment to implement a CAD system. Introduction of a CAD system without modification of existing procedures, equipment, and information flow, as well as decisions on the future development of automated information systems, could produce disastrous results.

The advent of computerization has created areas of concern that must be addressed before the design phase of a computer conversion program can be undertaken.

1. Local police presently collect a large amount of data with little or no reference to the objectives for which it is collected. That which is used relates only haphazardly to the needs of decision makers.
2. Much information required by police agencies is collected and stored elsewhere in local, county, regional, and/or statewide systems. Much of this information is currently unavailable, due to ignorance of its existence or to inappropriate mechanisms for its transfer.
3. Sufficient city and countywide computerization planning may not have been performed in order to prioritize and identify the relationships of a CAD system to the total long-range scheme of development.
4. Local CAD systems have yet to be thoroughly evaluated as operating subsystems within police agencies.

NEED FOR PLANNING

The primary objective of this chapter is to identify the tremendous amount of operational planning that must be performed before a competent decision can be made to implement a CAD system. The *operational planning* needed for implementing a CAD is addressed.

The ultimate result of the emphasis on planning is the development of a CAD system which will—

1. provide field personnel with immediate information for safety and effectiveness when dealing with field situations;
2. reduce the volume of reports and records, and organize information in such a manner that the system does not become overloaded with its own paperwork;
3. provide command dispatch personnel with accurate and complete information to direct and coordinate resources;
4. provide information requested by other public safety agencies, and retrieve similar information of local interest from other agencies.

POLICE AGENCY IMPLEMENTATION CONSIDERATIONS

In order to obtain an effective design and implementation plan for a CAD system, a four-task study plan and development program should be followed.

1. Definition of objectives; analysis of requirements and data sources
2. Determination of computer system specifications
3. Creation of conceptual computer system design
4. Preparation of computer implementation plan

DEFINITION OF OBJECTIVES:
ANALYSIS OF REQUIREMENTS AND DATA SOURCES

Before undertaking the actual study, the overall mission or objectives of the CAD system must be written and agreed upon by all of the affected parties. Not only will this clarify the direction which the study will take, but it will also establish a level of commitment that can be expected from each concerned person.

While a police agency is aware of the *basic* requirements of computerization as they apply to the CAD system, it is essential to begin the study by performing a comprehensive technical analysis of present and future data sources and user requirements to be imposed on the system. This procedure ensures that the system is directed to meeting the true requirements of a police agency.

In summary, this first task will provide an answer to the following questions:

1. What are the available data sources?
2. What are the required functions that the computer system must perform?

DETERMINATION OF COMPUTER SYSTEM SPECIFICATIONS

General user requirements form the basis for determining CAD specifications, which provide a detailed description of the structure of the system, including specifications in six separate areas (Sohn, 1975).

1. *System Output*—What information must the CAD system provide? What will be the form of the information? How frequently must it be available?
2. *Data Input*—What data must be available to the CAD system? What is its source, form, accuracy, and currency?
3. *Software*—What kinds of computer programs (if any) or new operating procedures must be developed? What quantitative or qualitative requirements must they meet? What support will be necessary from the data processing department for special software development (if required)?
4. *Hardware*—What types of computers (if any), peripheral equipment, or other physical equipment must be purchased, leased, or made available for the system? Will the agency's existing equipment be sufficient, or will other computer facilities be necessary?
5. *People*—How many people will be required to utilize the completed CAD system? What skills and skill-levels must be represented? Does the agency now have an adequate data-processing staff to meet the need? Are the Records and Communications sections of the law enforcement agency adequately staffed to handle the system?
6. *Interface*—What is necessary to interface with a city or county information System Master Plan (if any) and other operating or anticipated systems? What is the system relationship of the CAD system to any existing information systems? (Sohn, 1975).

The system requirements provide the basis for defining the outputs needed by the CAD system to meet the needs of the agency. In addition, the CAD system must be capable of preparing reports on a regularly scheduled basis to meet the periodic requirements of the agency. Another output area decision is the determination of the output conveyance methods available to the system, such as the cathode ray tube (video screen display). If a computerized system is found to be warranted, standard hard-copy printout should undoubtedly be available.

In addition to these key output requirement decisions, the needs or report requirements of the user divisions of the agency must be written as statements. These statements should include such parameters that would assist in command and control development for the following:

1. Types of reports
2. Number of reports

3. Report format
4. Report length
5. Frequency of report preparation
6. Number of copies
7. Sensitivity to time delays in report delivery
8. Sensitivity to data currency in the reports

The output information required by the user divisions determines the raw data *input* requirements into the system. In addition to identifying the necessary input elements, one must address the various data characteristics for each data element requiring accuracy, currency (frequency of update), and reliability. In addition to the characteristics of the data itself, the input requirements must be analyzed with respect to sources of data, format of data, mechanisms for storing data updating procedures, and responsibilities. Most of the data required for the CAD system may already be available from the dispatch operation. This varies depending upon the agency's philosophy toward a CAD system. Data not available may be obtained by expanding operating files to include additional data items, by creating new files containing the data items, or by resorting to special survey data.

The types of software that will be specialized for the system can be conveniently categorized into four groups

1. *Control software* — to ensure smooth and efficient system operation
2. *Manipulative software* — to extract, rearrange, and modify new input data, including file maintenance and data retrieval routines
3. *Display software* — to present information to user-agencies, utilizing preferred data formats and optimal display devices
4. *Analysis software* — (such as mathematical and statistical analysis programs) — to derive useful information from the police data base

In addition to specifying the software required for the system, an agency should investigate and evaluate existing CAD law enforcement packages to determine if they are applicable to the computer system.

Hardware specifications for the CAD computer system will relate to the adequacy of the agency's present system (if such exists).

"People" specifications relate to the manpower needs to operate the completed CAD system in terms of the number of personnel required, the type of skills needed, and the skill levels required.

It may be desirable to combine two or more of the "people requirements" into a specification for a single position. These positions should be developed in response to the existing capabilities available among the city's data-processing staff and the Records and Communication sections of the law enforcement agency. (Sohn, 1975).

CREATION OF CONCEPTUAL CAD SYSTEM DESIGN

The CAD conceptual system design is created to establish how the system will meet the requirements specified. The necessary hardware configuration for the CAD system should be described, and the memory requirements, processing speeds, and peripheral equipment fully identified. The design should include the structuring (in a broad sense) of the data file organization, including the identification of the data elements to be contained in the files and the determination of techniques for file initialization and update. Existing "off-the-shelf" CAD packages could be tentatively identified to meet the needs indicated in the software area, but preliminary designs of special software programs required for the system should also be included. The resulting conceptual system design and the system specifications should be fully documented and presented to the government body for approval.

A necessary part of this conceptual design task should be the consideration of cost/benefit factors. If a CAD system is indicated, it is particularly important to consider from a cost-versus-benefit viewpoint whether new equipment should be utilized or another alternative investigated.

PREPARATION OF A CAD SYSTEM IMPLEMENTATION PLAN

What is lacking at this point is a detailed plan outlining the steps that an agency should take to implement its conceived CAD system. It is strongly suggested that an agency follow a *phased system-implementation effort.*

For each task, the agency should develop an implementation schedule that will lead to a series of milestone completion points. At each milestone, the agency would have an operating CAD system that is one step more complete than that which was operational at the preceding milestone. Specific tasks should be listed in the implementation schedule, including hardware acquisition points, software completion times, and manpower loading points. In the early stages, the system may be quite modest in the sense that the automated data base is incomplete, sophisticated tools are unavailable, and only rudimentary display techniques are utilized. As system implementation continues, the data base expands — becoming more accurate, current, and complete. Additional analytical and display tools are made available. The important advantages of this phased approach are

1. Early system operational capability
2. Flexible design permitting controlled system growth
3. Stabilized flow of implementation funding (reduced front-end costs)
4. Simplicity of redirecting the system implementation as the department's needs change

The full implementation plan for the CAD system, including estimated costs and schedule, should be documented and presented for approval. This plan should include a determination of the expected costs of system development and identification of the anticipated benefits of system implementation. The cost-benefit analysis should be included.

After these tasks are completed, a summary of all task activities and results should be prepared, setting forth recommendations for the police computer system development and implementation.

Jerome Kanter provides some insight into the general management of a computer system (Kanter, 1977). Figure X-1 illustrates the role that should be played by top management, staff, and operating management. Police agencies would do well to pay close attention to these responsibilities in developing and implementing a CAD system.

PLANNING VENDOR SELECTION, EQUIPMENT, SOFTWARE, TRAINING, AND MAINTENANCE

The selection of a vendor to assist an agency in CAD system implementation means that the agency must carefully think through the process. A checklist should be developed that considers these five major categories

1. Vendor
2. Hardware
3. Software
4. Training and Installation
5. Maintenance/Service

The following checklist might prove useful to an agency desiring to implement a CAD system and to overcome some of the concerns evident in the analysis of research findings in the preceding chapter.

Vendor

1. How long has the company (vendor) been in business?

   Less than 2 years
   2–5 years
   5–10 years
   More than 10 years

2. How many computer systems has the company (vendor) installed?

   Less than 50
   50–150
   150–300
   Over 300

Top Management	Staff Management	Operating Management
Concern with overall objectives; explain what is essential; ensure an understanding; monitor to see that the understanding and awareness are present.	Awareness and participation in establishment of external/internal strategies. Middle management is cognizant of the effect of these policies on actual law enforcement operations.	Develop and produce procedure manuals. Train people in use of system. Make necessary preparations for the conversion and transition period. Should be on call to handle detailed questions or respond to specific issues.
Ensure that external/internal strategies are understood, e.g., all application areas must take into account the financial requirements; applications must be built on the assumption that law enforcement conditions will change.	Participate in development of the overall system specifications. Representation on advisory committee. Involvement in subsystems that affect the manager's division or affects those divisions with whom he interfaces (i.e., records, patrol, communications).	Help establish psychological atmosphere for acceptance and cooperation of operating people involved. Develop outlook that emphasizes that system benefits will offset the effort to change and transaction.
Participate in establishing and reviewing integrated system specifications; this is overall game plan—the framework or road map. Should have opportunity to review any major system changes.	Obtain proper people involvement by setting the proper example. Middle management is not concerned with specific system design but the issues discussed and reviewed at advisory committee meetings will impact design.	Explain where the individual parts or roles of operating people fit into total CAD picture. Maintain positive motivation. Ensure that system operates according to specification—feedback any discrepancies or problems.
Participate in establishing overall schedule. Review major milestones and project status.	Assign analysts within a particular area or at least provide contact point, an individual who can speak for the department or perspective to know when middle management should be called in to approve a major issue.	

Figure X-1. General management involvement in a CAD system. Source: Jerome Kanter, *Management-Oriented Information Systems*, 2nd Edition. (Englewood Cliffs, New Jersey: Prentice-Hall, 1977).

3. How many service locations does the company (vendor) have?

1–25
25–50
Over 50

4. How much of the total system will the company (vendor) provide?

Equipment
Training
Installation
Servicing
Programming

5. Will the company quote all costs separately? (Hardware, software, supplies, service, training, etc.) Everything—including costs—should be in writing! The last thing you need is to discover "hidden costs."

Yes   Some   No

6. Does the company accept full responsibility for the following?

Presale system analysis	Yes	Some	No
Postsale detail system analysis	Yes	Some	No
System design	Yes	Some	No
Programming	Yes	Some	No
System installation	Yes	Some	No

7. Will the company provide—and commit itself to—a full implementation schedule? If not, who will do what part?

Equipment delivery	Yes	No
Installation	Yes	No
Software delivery	Yes	No
Training		

8. After the system is installed, how much on-going responsibility (such as software maintenance) will the company retain?

Total Minimal None

Hardware—Central Processing Unit (CPU)

1. Is the CPU cycle speed quoted in . . .Specific cycle times have a great effect on system throughput; in fact, any CPU doing business processing spends most of its time "waiting" for input/output tasks to be completed—a very important consideration in CAD systems.

Nanoseconds?
Microseconds 1 to 1.5?
Microseconds more than 1.5?

2. Does the CPU have automatic restart logic in the event of a power failure?

Yes   No

3. How much memory is available in the CPU? What are your CAD requirements?

Minimum _____K
Maximum _____K

4. If CRT stations are added to the system, does each one require a segment (partition) of core memory? If so, how much?

Yes   No

5. Does the CPU have the logic or checking ability to warn a maintenance engineer when an electrical component is intermittent or beginning to fail?

Yes   No

6. How many clean or dedicated lines (if any) are needed? (A common hidden cost.)

1
2 or more

Hardware—Mass Storage Unit (Disk Storage)

The mass-storage unit, called "disk storage," determines how much information you can have on-line. Every unit has a limitation. What are your needs now? Five years from now? If your processing needs continue to grow with your CAD system, consider the ease and costs of expanding the mass-storage unit.

1. How many disk drives can be added to increase mass storage?	3 or more 1 None
2. What types of mass-storage units can be added?	Disk Diskette
3. What is the disk drive capacity?	10 MB or more 8–9 MB 5–7 MB 1–4 MB Less than 1 MB
4. If the disk data storage covers multiple disk (not diskette) surfaces, are they . . . Removing the disk makes copying and backing up of data a lot easier. If the disk drive does *not* accomodate a "split pack" (part fixed, part removable), a second drive or a tape drive is required for backing up data . . . and that means additional expenses.	All removable? Removable and fixed? All fixed?

Hardware—CRT Stations

1. How many video display work stations can be added to the CAD system?	8 or more 4–7 2–3 1 None
2. How many characters can be displayed at one time? What are your CAD requirements?	1,980 or more 1,920 960 480 240
3. How fast does the display unit transfer data to/from the central processing unit (CPU)?	960 cps 480 240 120 Less than 120

4. Can the CRT display unit be located in a   Yes   No
   different room or building than the basic
   system?

Hardware—Printers

1. Does the company offer different types of   Yes   No
   printers?
2. Can more than one printer be incorporated   3 or more
   into the system at the same time?   2

                                          No
3. If the company suggests a single character   150 or more   80
   printer how fast will it print characters per   45 30
   second?   10
4. If you change printers is there any cost   No   Some   Yes
   beyond the price of the new printer? If so,
   how much?
5. Can the printer provide multiple copies?   6 or more   No
                                          2–4

Software

Basically, there are two types of software:
- *Systems software*—the control program which coordinates the various "hardware" elements of the system—sometimes referred to as the "operating system;"
- *Applications software*—those programs which are developed to accomplish an agency's specific CAD jobs.
  1. Will the company's own staff support and   Company
     maintain the operating system or will your   Agency
     agency do it?
  2. If there is a future problem ("bug") with   Yes   No
     the operating system, will the company
     correct the problem at no cost?
  3. Is this part of the written contract?   Yes   No
  4. Is the company proposing custom or stan-   Yes   No
     dard CAD ("packaged") software for your   Custom   Standard
     applications?
  5. Will the company survey and ana-   Yes   No
     lyze your application requirements and
     submit a written proposal outlining the
     necessary modifications of its package to
     meet your needs, along with a fixed-price
     quote for the modified package?

6. Will the company warrant the application software installed on your system to perform *as specified?*

    Yes No
    With time limit

7. Will the company demonstrate live, installable CAD application programs before you sign a contract?

    Yes No

8. If you have a signed contract (assuming you do not already have your own programming staff) . . .

    Who is responsible for the systems analysis and design work?

    Company staff
    Third party

    Who is responsible for the actual programming?

    Company staff
    Third party

9. Who is responsible for CAD application program installation?

    Company staff
    Third party

10. Will you see the entire system and CAD applications demonstrated using "life data" prior to taking delivery?

    Yes No

11. Prior to equipment delivery, will the conversion of data to your CAD computerized system be

    Scheduled (firm dates in writing)? With costs quoted and written? With responsibility for handling it all specifically assigned?

    Yes No
    Yes No
    Yes No

12. Does the company fully document the applications so that they are understandable to you or another party?

    Yes No

13. Does the company quote the cost of *all* software—including custom modifications—separately from the hardware costs in its proposal?

    Yes No

Training and Installation

1. Who will be responsible for system installation and operator training?

    Company
    Third party
    Your agency

2. Does the company provide installation reference manuals?

    Yes No

3. Once the system is delivered, how many specific installation personnel will the company assign?

    2 or more None
    One

4. Will you have the same installation person-   Yes No
   nel for the duration of the installation?
5. How many of these CAD systems have the   10 or more   None
   installation personnel previously installed?   Under 10
6. Will the company provide and commit itself   Yes No
   to a written implementation schedule—a
   phased plan for installing the system?
7. Are all operating instructions *fully docu-*   Yes No
   mented and understandable by the operators
   being trained?
8. Does the company offer formal classroom
   training to your personnel in . . .
   System operation?   Yes No
   Application programming?   Yes No
9. Does the company provide training for   Yes No
   management and supervisory personnel?

Maintenance/Service

1. Who will provide maintenance for your   Company
   system?   Third Party
       Your Agency
2. If maintenance is not supplied by company,   Yes No
   does the maintenance group service the
   company's equipment exclusively?
3. Will your maintenance contract be with a   Company
   third party or with the company?   Third party
4. Does the service contract completely de-   Yes Some No
   lineate all services to be provided?
5. Is service available locally, under control   Yes No
   of the company's management?
6. What is the company's average response   1–4 hrs. 5–8 hrs.
   time for service?   1–2 days
       Over 2 days
7. How often is preventive maintenance per-   Monthly Quarterly
   formed?   Semiannually
       3X/Year
       Never
8. How much will such "routine" maintenance   Less than 5% of system
   cost?   price
       5 to 10%
       Over 10%

9. Are there any "extra" maintenance services   No   Some   Yes
   not included in the maintenance contract?

This chapter has tried to point out some of the crucial operational planning steps that are necessary in planning a CAD system. If you are selecting a vendor to assist you, the checklist should provide a necessary starting point for negotiation. The success or failure of a system can well depend upon

1. Definition of objectives
2. Analysis of requirements

Furthermore, it outlines specific examples of the planning considerations and the steps involved to prepare police agencies for a successful and effective CAD implementation. Agencies must recognize the need for and importance of clarifying goals and expectations, coping with change, providing necessary training and carefully developing implementation plans. These operational planning concerns must be addressed whether planning a CAD system or developing a crime analysis strategy or a special events plan.

TOPICS FOR DISCUSSION

1. Define operational planning.
2. Describe the operational planning environment as related to a criminal justice agency.
3. Why is it important to know your objective?
4. The following lists consists of areas that might be addressed by an operational plan. Choose one and apply the operational planning steps you would implement to address the area.
   a. A major parade
   b. Armed robberies of convenience stores
   c. New job performance rating system
   d. Personnel management computer system
   e. Vehicle use and allocation system

REFERENCES

Kanter, J. *Management-Oriented Management Information Systems*, 2nd ed. Englewood Cliffs, N.J.: Prentice-Hall, 1977, p. 149.

O'Neill, Michael. The acceptance and implementation of computer-aided dispatch systems by local police agencies. Unpublished doctoral dissertation, S.F., CA: Golden Gate University, May, 1980, pp. 72–98.

O'Reilly, Charles. Variations in decision makers' use of information sources: The impact of quality and accessibility of information. *Academy of Management Journal*, December 1982, 756–71.

Rivera, G., and others. Managerial information processing: A research review. *Administrative Science Quarterly.* March, 1981, pp. 116–34.

Sherman, Philip. *Strategic Planning for Technology Industries,* Reading, Mass: Addison-Wesley, 1982.

Sohn, R. L., et al. *Application of Computer-Aided Dispatch in Law Enforcement: An Introductory Planning Guide,* Pasadena, CA: Jet Propulsion Laboratory, December 1975, p. 13.

INDEX